A Life More Noble

A Life More Noble

First published by Octavia in 2015.

Octavia
Emily House
202-208 Kensal Road
London
W10 5BN

T 020 8354 5500
E info@octavia.org.uk
W www.octavia.org.uk

ISBN 9780957307315

Printed in Great Britain by The Printing House.

Design and layout by Avenue Design Ltd
www.avenuelondon.co.uk

CONTENTS

PREFACE

D eciding how to celebrate the 150th anniversary of the first housing acquired by Octavia Hill – one of the great Victorian philanthropists – was a puzzle. She already has a memorial in Westminster Abbey and naming another building after her or producing a timeline of events felt like a rather tired approach to commemorating someone with her breadth of thought and ambition.

Gillian Darley concludes her biography with a quote from Octavia:

> *'When I am gone, I hope my friends will not try*
> *to carry out any special system or to follow blindly in the*
> *track which I have trodden. New circumstances require*
> *various efforts and it is the spirit and not the dead form*
> *that should be perpetuated.'*

With this in mind, we decided to explore what had happened to that 'spirit' and in late 2013 started a project to explore the contemporary relevance of her ideas.

In 1893, Octavia wrote congratulating her friend, the Reverend Ingham Brookes, when he announced that he was to be married. Buried deep within the letter is a phrase which, as Julia Unwin explains in her article on page 206, could serve brilliantly as a mission statement for most charities, housing associations and public bodies in the UK today. Octavia wrote to Brookes:

*'...all of our work together is to make **individual life noble, homes happy and family life good.**'*

Our aim was to find out what relevance, if any, that phrase might have in 21st-century Britain. We knew that the book would be more widely read if we gained the support of some well-known figures but were surprised by the very personal and visceral responses that Octavia's 'noble life' phrase elicited. The general willingness and enthusiasm of everyone to engage was, of itself, a strong indicator that the idea we were exploring remains relevant.

We also wanted the perspective of those who are as close to following in Octavia's housing footsteps as we could find. True Londoners. So we spoke to a cross-section of staff members and residents of the inner London housing association that bears Octavia's name; their comments give a different slant to what a contemporary Octavia Hill might be thinking about.

The various pieces which follow are unashamedly diverse. They capture the ideas as they unfolded in discussions – they are not measured blocks of public relations material but freely-given articles and records of what we were told. Individually, they each tell a story but taken together – as with much of the work that Octavia Hill did in a variety of fields – they give a stronger, richer, more complex narrative.

The articles are only loosely structured around a number of themes. We start with a piece of graphic art that gives a flavour of one writer's journey in contributing to this book. The scene-setting continues with a piece written by Octavia herself followed by overviews of her life from Ian Hislop and Gillian Darley.

In the pieces that follow we take Octavia's lead and start with housing. There are articles on the problems of housing policy from Campbell Robb, Isabel Hardman, Lord Best and David Orr interwoven with discussion, interviews and comments from Octavia Housing residents, board members and staff.

But the provision of buildings was only the start of Octavia Hill's work and the themes in this book move into care for the elderly and the need for accessible open space. We also look at the importance of individual example in gaining a perspective on what a noble life means (including pieces from Tamsin Greig, Sandy Toksvig and Peter Tatchell) simply because, for Octavia Hill, personal example mattered. We have also included pieces by befrienders (volunteers who spend time with isolated or vulnerable people), the views of some of the people they befriend and pieces by academics and thinkers on some of the wider perspectives of what makes for a noble or happy life.

Throughout the book and the various articles several contributors refer to the importance of 'community' – the responsibility of one person for others. A number of residents speak of the loss of a feeling of community, and the Rt Hon. Alan Johnson MP and Charlie Phillips in particular speak of their experience of just how strong a sense of community there was in Notting Hill in times past.

We also have pieces on the importance of open space (including one from Sir Simon Jenkins) and comments from Sir Crispin Tickell on the environmental consequences of our current approach to development. In addition, we have articles on entrepreneurship from Deborah Meaden and John Bird. These are all areas in which Octavia Hill made important contributions.

Through speaking to so many individuals in the compilation of this book, it became clear that many people were reluctant to use the word 'noble' in relation to their ambitions or values. If you substitute it with the word 'dignity', however, there is almost universal acceptance that this constitutes a basic human need. The Rt Hon. Lord Howard, as Chair of Hospice UK, talks about dignity in dying while Octavia resident Steve Smith speaks about the importance of hope and Jean Roch, another of our residents, speaks of being ashamed as the opposite of being noble. Such responses underline the truly subjective nature of a noble life.

Attempting to give some shape to the contributions we received runs the risk of flattening the subtlety of what is a very rich picture of how our contributors see the issue of nobility, happy homes and family life. There are contributions that argue for housing reform or education or open spaces as the chief legacy of Octavia Hill while others focus on the more generic categories of community spirit and support for others. For me, it is the overarching nature of her uniting vision of shared, mixed communities, in which responsibility for self and for others really matters, that comes through as her greatest contribution.

This book was an experiment. When we started we had no idea what we would find. It is not a tightly-argued case for action, nor is it a closely-argued academic thesis to be defended. Rather, it is a collection of pieces compiled by some latter-day disciples of Ms Hill's obvious common sense as a tribute to her work and ambition.

One hundred and fifty years on, is her ambition still relevant? We think so. And, as Cathy Newman says in the final piece:

> *'Octavia Hill once spoke of "mighty issues of the new and better days to come". Octavia, there is no shortage of mighty issues you would have liked to have grappled within 21st-century Britain.'*

Grahame Hindes

Chief Executive, Octavia,
London, September 2015

JOHN-PAUL FLINTOFF

John-Paul Flintoff is an author, journalist and member
of the faculty of The School of Life.

OCTAVIA HILL

Extract taken from Four Years' Management
of a London Court; first published in *Macmillan's Magazine*,
July 1869. In this, Octavia is describing her work in Freshwater
Place, Marylebone, houses acquired by John Ruskin and placed
under her management.

About four years ago I was put in possession of three
houses in one of the worst courts in Marylebone. Six
other houses were bought subsequently. All were crowded
with inmates. The first thing to be done was to put them
in decent tenantable order. The set last purchased was a
row of cottages facing a bit of desolate ground, occupied
with wretched, dilapidated cow-sheds, manure heaps, old
timber, and rubbish of every description. The houses were
in a most deplorable condition – the plaster was dropping
from the walls; on one staircase a pail was placed to catch
the rain that fell through the roof. All the staircases were
perfectly dark; the banisters were gone, having been burnt
as firewood by tenants. The grates, with large holes in
them, were falling forward into the rooms.

The wash-house, full of lumber belonging to the landlord, was locked up; thus the inhabitants had to wash clothes, as well as to cook, eat, and sleep in their small rooms. The dustbin, standing in the front of the houses, was accessible to the whole neighbourhood, and boys often dragged from it quantities of unseemly objects and spread them over the court. The state of the drainage was in keeping with everything else. The pavement of the backyard was all broken up, and great puddles stood in it so that the damp crept up the outer walls. One large but dirty water-butt received the water laid on for the houses; it leaked, and for such as did not fill their jugs when the water came in, or who had no jugs to fill, there was no water. The former landlord's reply to one of the tenants who asked him to have an iron hoop put round the butt to prevent leakage, was, that 'if he didn't like it' (i.e. things as they were) 'he might leave'. The man to whom this was spoken – by far the best tenant in the place – is now with us, and often gives his spare time to making his room more comfortable, knowing that he will be retained, if he behaves well.

This landlord was a tradesman in a small way of business – not a cruel man, except in so far as variableness of dealing is cruelty; but he was a man without capital to spend on improvements, and lost an immense percentage of his rent by bad debts. I went over the houses with him the last day he collected his rents there, that he might introduce me to the people as the owner of the property. He took a man with him, whom, as he confided to me, he wished to pass off upon the people as a broker. It was evident that, whether they saw through this deceit or not, they had no experience which led them to believe he intended to carry into effect the threats he uttered. The arrears of rent were enormous. I had been informed that the honest habitually pay for the dishonest, the owner relying upon their payments to compensate for all losses; but I was amazed to find to what an extent this was the case. Six, seven, or eight weeks' rent was due from most tenants, and in some cases very much more; whereas, since I took possession of the houses (of which I collect the rents each week myself) I have never allowed a second week's rent to become due.

I think no one who has not experienced it can fully realise the almost awed sense of joy with which one enters upon such a possession as that above described, conscious of having the power to set it, even partially, in order.

IAN HISLOP

A few years ago I made a documentary called *Age of the Do-Gooders* to reclaim that pejorative term and reappraise the reputations of some of the great reformers of the Victorian age. Octavia Hill was one of those I profiled and, like many of them, she was both brilliant and brittle, inspiring and infuriating, dogmatic and yet an undeniable force for good. I focused, in particular, on her compassionate yet hard-headed approach to social housing, where she demonstrated a characteristic mixture of idealism and pragmatism. Anyone insisting on 'order, cleanliness and self-respect' from those who had lived in London's worst slums was aiming high – but it worked.

I interviewed a long-term resident of a property owned by Octavia, the descendant of Hill's own organisation, and he told me about the 'strict but fair' ladies who inspected the properties and tried to make sure that social housing (and its occupants) remained 'decent'. He called them 'disciples of Octavia Hill' and talked enthusiastically of 'high standards'.

Housing was, however, just one area in which Hill made a contribution to national life but the remarkable thing about her was not just her breadth of interest but the depth of it. Her aims were certainly 'noble' yet they were firmly rooted in reality. Like many others, she had read about London's poor but then she went and acted on first-hand experience. Victorian women often became involved in charity largely because they were excluded from traditional professions and routes to influence, and charitable work enabled them to make a genuine difference to society. It was respectable for middle-class women to worry about poverty, particularly in the domestic sphere, and Hill turned this to her advantage in realising that her initiatives in the field of what we would now call 'welfare' had an effect on other spheres of life. She worked hard and, despite repeatedly suffering from exhaustion, she bestowed a huge legacy. When I think of her I always recall the figure described by George Eliot at the end of *Middlemarch* who may not be a great heroine but who works in unseen channels for the greater good of all:

But the effect of her being on those around her was incalculably diffusive: for the growing good of the world is partly dependent on unhistoric acts; and that things are not so ill with you and me as they might have been is half owing to the number who lived faithfully a hidden life, and rest in unvisited tombs.

I hope Octavia Hill is not forgotten and that she remains a source of inspiration. She was, of course, deeply religious and this motivated her in her desire to 'make individual lives noble'. Even though we are uneasy nowadays with her religious views and uneasy even with the word 'noble', if you substitute 'noble' with 'dignified' and talk of 'giving people their dignity' I think it is pretty clear that her vision is as relevant now as ever.

Ian Hislop is a writer, journalist and broadcaster. He has been editor of satirical magazine *Private Eye* since 1986 and is a team captain on the BBC show *Have I Got News for You*.

THE INCOME MANAGEMENT TEAM

What does 'noble' mean to you?

Niki: I think of knights!

Akinola: That's the first thing that comes to mind but I think in this day and age, it means decent. 'Noble' translates to 'decent' nowadays. In the context of what Octavia talked about in terms of noble lives, she just wanted them to live a decent life. A life where you have all the basics: roof, shelter, job.

Osei: I think it's to do with class.

Akinola: It's about the social contract. The social contract between you and society. Think of Rousseau, Hobbes…

Mary: Well, it's associated with money and richness,

I think. It makes me think of years ago, rich people… the landed gentry.

Breda: Like the people in Downton Abbey!

Niki, Akinola, Osei, Mary and **Breda** work in
the Income Management team at Octavia,
helping tenants pay their rent.

GILLIAN DARLEY

Every one of the contributors to this book recognises some measure of indebtedness to Octavia Hill and her work, many aspects of which have endured, albeit with necessary adjustments, into the 21st century. As her biographer, I can trace the influences upon her own life and achievements while I leave it to others to trace her legacy, as it has endured.

Briefly put, the circumstances of her early life prepared her almost immediately for difficulty. Her father's bankruptcy (and, soon, his enforced removal from the family) meant that as a very small child she shared a peripatetic existence with her mother, now a single parent, and her siblings.

Born in 1838, Octavia was the eighth daughter of James Hill, an East Anglian grain merchant, brewer and banker but, more importantly for the family's future, an Owenite idealist who lost everything for the cause. His wife, born Caroline Southwood Smith, had come to Wisbech as governess for his older children. She was already a published writer on educational theory and a staunch advocate of radical, Pestalozzian, methods of schooling. Her father, Dr Thomas Southwood Smith, was a leading public health campaigner, an advocate of social action on housing, child labour and a dozen other topics. He lived in a liberal, feminist social circle in Highgate, cohabiting with sisters Margaret and Mary Gillies, artist and author respectively. Once Caroline had settled back in London, by now with five girls of her own, Dr Southwood Smith took a large part in their lives, even adopting one granddaughter, Gertrude. Octavia Hill's upbringing was, self evidently, a departure from the usual middle-class childhood of the time.

In London, Caroline became manager of the toymakers of the Ladies Cooperative Guild – a short-lived initiative aimed at married women without other means of support. Soon Octavia was helping, particularly with their children, and saw for herself the dire reality of the London poor, living in courts and rookeries around Holborn and St Giles, in the early 1850s. Exposed to these almost unimaginable scenes, she began to consider what she might do to alleviate their poverty. Through the Ladies Guild she met John Ruskin and also the leaders of the Christian Socialist group. She soon realised that rapacious landlords were a root cause of poverty; they left their housing to rot while they continued to press for rent, on pain of eviction. John Ruskin became her main source of support in these years, employing her as a fine art copyist so that she had a regular source of income and, on inheriting his family fortune, buying the first terrace of cottages for Octavia's 'scheme'. Her idea was to renovate housing, with and around the tenants, and make the rent collection a pretext to pay regular and supportive visits to the families – an early form of social work. Paradise Place, Marylebone, now Garbutt Place, was the first, followed by Freshwater Place (also bought by Ruskin). They were the first seeds of what became a complex network of property, maintained and overseen by a growing army of volunteer rent collectors. From the beginning, Ruskin expected a five per cent return on his investment.

While the enterprise expanded, and colleagues such as Emma Cons and Henrietta Barnett took the 'Octavia Hill method' to other parts of London, Octavia continually reinforced the different elements that she brought to her tenants: improved housing went with playgrounds; access to outdoors led to public open space, both small and large; opportunities for work allowed for regular rent payments which, in turn, led to self-respect; and the public art and entertainment she provided for tenants' groups all fell within her notion of a better life. Although her own religious faith was the backbone of what she did, she had no prescriptive views or evangelical tendencies.

She gained her support and, gradually, her renown, through a combination of means. Young women came to work alongside her or her colleagues as volunteer rent collectors, while others, a growing network of influential individuals, purchased properties for her to manage or gave a regular annual donation to support the work. As time went on, she ensured that what she did, and her observations, were often documented. She began her Letters to Fellow-workers in 1877, an annual newsletter for her supporters, for their eyes only. Elsewhere she followed her mother's example by writing for leading periodicals, with essays on her observations being published at intervals and, no doubt, read by people in authority. Her topics included not only housing conditions but also the lack of public open space where the poor were concentrated, the failures as well as the successes of her work and, in some detail, the human face of her 'method'.

As her experience grew and, with it, her need to delegate and to consider the bigger picture, Octavia Hill was shrewd at targeting powerful people. In 1884, she was a key witness to the Royal Commission on the Housing of the Working Classes. Small and dogged as she was, with – apparently – a mellifluous speaking voice, she grew fearless, and increasingly effective, in addressing large audiences. By the time that she had become a co-founder of the National Trust (1895), alongside Sir Robert Hunter and Canon Hardwicke Rawnsley, her presence on a platform, appealing for a given site, or cause, was a sure guarantee of success.

If her own preferences hardened to include clearly-targeted charity, an antipathy to municipal authorities and disbelief in the old age pension or the franchise for women, she also opened the doors to women in dozens of professions – beginning with housing management – and she transformed the world of housing, social work, access to art and open space. Octavia, by default, wrote her own obituary in 1898. As she said on the occasion of the presentation of John Singer Sargent's portrait of her, she did not want to leave behind systems, organisations or formulas but, essentially, 'greater ideals, greater hope and patience to realise both'.

Gillian Darley is a writer. Her book *Octavia Hill: Social Reformer and Founder of the National Trust* (2010) is a comprehensive biography of Octavia Hill.

DAVE AND LORRAINE BURFORD

Lorraine: I don't think Octavia Hill wanted to make people into noblemen or anything like that. No, she wanted to take them away from the rough life into a nicer life.

Dave: Yes, she wanted to make people's life better really, to get them out of the gutter, help people get on in life and help the poor feel great for themselves. I come from a big family. When I was young, we lived in a small house; three rooms it had, and a scullery. Octavia wanted to get people out of that kind of environment and into houses with baths and things.

Lorraine: It's a great help having somewhere decent to live. It's no good being overcrowded in one small house. We didn't always have a bathroom did we, even in Prince's Place?

Dave: It's a lot different nowadays to when we first started out. We used to have to go down the baths and have a wash.

It was about a mile away! It made a difference when we moved into Crossways in 1973 – they were luxurious flats and there was even a place to connect a washing machine. We moved out of a three-room house with no bath or nothing – and an outside toilet – into a place with a bath and shower and everything.

Lorraine: Yes, it had everything. Lovely.

Dave: There's a different atmosphere around now. Years ago, a tenant in the flats used to run day trips, residents' coach outings, and things like that. Everybody used to get on but nowadays people don't mix. They don't say 'Good morning' or anything like that as you go past. A lot of people don't even know their next-door neighbours.

Lorraine: The nice thing round here is that our next-door neighbours and Jean upstairs – we all used to live in the same street. I even went to school with Jean's brothers.

Dave: As a caretaker, even when I've worked so many hours in the morning, if I see paper blowing about I pick it up and if people see me do that, they don't drop paper so the place keeps quite clean.

Lorraine: It's fulfilling being able to keep it nice where you live.

Dave: People appreciate having a caretaker. They feel safe and all that. Round here, we tell each other when we are going away so we can keep an eye out when the houses are empty. Or if someone has got a parcel coming, you don't mind taking it in. It's all about community, really.

Dave and **Lorraine Burford** live in Holland Park. Both have worked as caretakers for Octavia. Dave has worked as a caretaker for 47 years, making him the organisation's longest-serving member of staff.

THE RT HON. ALAN JOHNSON MP

A s a child in early 1950s North Kensington I was unaware of the enormous political and social challenges facing post-war Britain. I certainly didn't regard the houses we lived in as slums, or feel that we were particularly unfortunate, but the houses on our street were very different to the ones my mother cleaned for a living in South Kensington. During school holidays she'd take my sister and me with her to work. The houses she cleaned were grand and, understandably, many of the occupants were irritated at the prospect of a pair of ragamuffins playing in their elegant drawing rooms. If we were allowed in, we'd watch my mother on a chair stretching high to dust or kneeling to scrub, scrape and polish.

Linda and I didn't expect to live in such houses. Their occupants were from a different world connected only peripherally to ours. The people whose houses my mother cleaned owned their homes whilst everybody in Southam Street, London W10 rented, so far as we knew. The families who shared our front door would come and go, just as we came and went; from 107 to 149 Southam Street and from there to 6 Walmer Road. Some of our neighbours rented from what I later heard described as slum landlords, the most notorious of whom was Peter Rachman, but we were with the Rowe (later Octavia) Housing Trust, something my mother told us we should be eternally thankful for. Her dream was to live in a house with her own front door; a release from our shared accommodation with no bathroom, no running hot water and a dilapidated outside toilet.

While we waited for my mother's dream to be fulfilled, the Trust met our needs, moving us from one room to three and then, even after my father had left us, to four rooms. My mother even persuaded them to install a bath and copper boiler in one corner of the decrepit basement with brown formica boards around it – our first bathroom.

My mother may have neglected to tell the Trust that her husband had deserted her for fear of not getting a bigger dwelling – I don't know. What I do know is that whilst she acquired many debts she always paid the rent on time.

Rowe/Octavia had an office on Portobello Road (known to locals as The Lane). My mother would 'go up The Lane' every week to hand the money to a clerk who would initial the rent book. I can still picture that office; cream woodwork, brown lino and a strong smell of disinfectant.

Battered by ill fortune and dogged by poor health, my mother's basic human need for shelter had at least been met and she wasn't going to let that slip away. Rowe/Octavia was our source of security – a 'trust' in more ways than one. We three were just a few of the many people over the years who have relied on its services and been thankful for its existence.

Alan Johnson is the Labour Member of Parliament for Hull West and Hussle. He is a former Home Secretary and Shadow Chancellor.

"IF PEOPLE FEEL A
SENSE OF BELONGING,
THEY WILL HAVE
RESPECT AND CARE
FOR THE PEOPLE
AND PLACES
AROUND THEM."

Maxine Peake

RITA POWELL

We called our landladies 'the ladies' – they used to come and collect our rent and make sure we looked after the place. They were quite strict. There was one time when a woman next door didn't have any net curtains up and, one day, one of the ladies knocked on our door and asked us if we'd tell our neighbour if she'd mind putting some net curtains up. She said: 'I shall be writing to her, but in the meantime would you tell her to put some curtains up so that passers by don't think that the house is empty.' Some of the ladies were ever so kind. When my little 'uns were small, the ladies used to give us a half a crown savings stamp for the children. My sister-in-law said that once, when her dad was ill, the ladies would come round and bring half a dozen eggs and some butter for them.

Rita Powell is an Octavia resident living in Gable Cottages, a late 19th-century residence designed using Octavia Hill's own vision in Southwark. She has lived there for 49 years.

LILLIAN BRYANT

I remember my first home during World War I. I couldn't have been more than four or five but it's stuck in my mind all these years. We lived in a two-up, two-down place and when the sirens went and the Zeppelins came overhead, we sat in the hallway for, you know, for safety.

I feel privileged to have got to the age of 103. The only thing is, it's lonely. I should have got used to it by now, but I haven't really. I don't like the weekends. They seem so long and I don't see anybody – sometimes for about three days. I'm not friendly with my neighbours. If it wasn't for the Wednesday Club I wouldn't go out at all during the week. I live each day as it comes – that's my philosophy.

Lillian Bryant lives in St John's Wood and has lived in London all her life. At 103, she is currently the oldest person using the Octavia Foundation's befriending service.

THE RT HON.
THE BARONESS GREENGROSS

O ctavia Hill firmly believed that good homes make for better lives and, in the mid-19th century, her theory of housing fostered a spirit of cooperation between tenant and landlord – the landlord to provide a habitable property, and the tenant to maintain it. However, despite the efforts of her, and others like her, housing poverty levels remained stubbornly high and some pockets of it still remain today.

So, how well have Octavia's values withstood the test of time and how relevant are they to a diverse, multicultural Britain, with an ageing demographic, where government cuts and external pressures have created significant challenges for the housing sector? Well, they are certainly still relevant, but much still remains to be done. Relative poverty after housing costs (households with less than 60 per cent of median income) has remained at around 21 per cent since the mid-1990s and our housing stock is, if anything, deteriorating. Therefore, unless government policy can be translated into the delivery of new homes, or the regeneration of empty homes, we won't be able to house the five million additional households likely to be created within the next two decades.

But what about 'nobility'? Regarding Octavia's aspiration of a 'noble' life for the individual, how practical is that in the 21st century? Today, I think we would rather use the term 'dignified' to describe the way a person should be treated, especially if they are old and infirm. We would all want to maintain our dignity in that situation but, unfortunately, all too often in modern UK care situations the first things to fall by the wayside are personal dignity and respect − so there is still a fair way to go before that hope is fulfilled.

For Octavia, a happy and good life would be one free from Beveridge's 'five giant evils' − squalor, ignorance, want, idleness and disease − which were the driving force behind the great education and welfare reforms of the mid-20th century, and the aims of which have, largely, been achieved. However, in the modern western world, personal 'happiness' and contentment levels, rather than being value driven by what the philosopher Alain de Botton calls an 'epicurean' acquisition list of private friendships, freedom of thought and health or wellbeing, are all too often driven by the immediate satisfaction obtained by the acquisition of material possessions – cars, houses and other luxury ephemera – rather than any considerations of good personal behaviour or of satisfying the needs and wants of other people.

So, all in all, I think we could reasonably give ourselves only seven out of ten for the leading of a 'noble' life and the following of basic decent principles such as 'do as you would be done by'. If, going forward, we set the determination to treat each other with dignity and respect in all our business and social dealings as our cornerstone, then we would greatly increase our chances of building a decent civil society within which to lead noble lives.

Baroness Greengross has been a member of the House of Lords since 2000. She was Director General of Age Concern England from 1987 until 2000 and is now President of the International Longevity Centre – UK.

MAXINE PEAKE

When asked by the *Evening Standard* earlier this year who your London hero was, you said Octavia Hill. Why does she inspire you?

I had always been intrigued by the Octavia Hill properties near Waterloo and it was only by seeking out who she was about ten years ago that I became aware of Octavia and her work. What I admire about her most is her vision and her work ethic. She was an enabler – she helped people to help themselves. She promoted the importance of self-improvement, education, the arts and the idea that, ultimately, people will give respect when they feel respected. Tantamount to this is a sense of community and belonging, and Octavia provided this by encouraging recreation and access to open spaces for the masses. Octavia was extremely driven, a visionary. There is something noble and fearless about her that I am drawn to.

What do you think Octavia Hill would make of the UK's current social and economic climate?

I think she'd be horrified by the conditions some people have to endure in modern society. I certainly am. We are in a dreadful state regarding social housing and welfare. One of the many terrible things that Margaret Thatcher did was to create the right to buy; it contributed to our shocking housing shortage and this issue hasn't been properly addressed by subsequent governments. And landlords up and down the country are allowed to charge ridiculously overpriced rents on properties that are not fit for purpose.

Many poor people are vilified by the media and by politicians, and this bullying, scapegoating behaviour has a knock-on effect where people feel that they have slipped off the social scale; that they have no future and no hope. It's criminal.

Octavia was a big believer in promoting a sense of community. What does the idea of community mean to you?

A sense of community is vital. If people feel a sense of belonging, they will have respect and care for the people and places all around them. They will feel safe and hopeful. We are all social creatures and we need to engage with others. Community is about security, boundaries and people looking out for each other. It's a support network, an extended family.

Can culture and the arts have an 'ennobling' effect on people?

The arts are an essential part of life. By having the opportunity to express ourselves, we can respect ourselves and others. The arts provide a way for us to find our voice, our individuality, and self-expression is vital to a full life. Everyone should have access to cultural activities and no one understood that more than Octavia. She brought music, art and nature into the lives of ordinary working people.

What issues would Octavia Hill need to address today?

Unfortunately, I think she would need to address the same issues that she tackled during her lifetime. The rich are getting richer and the poor are getting poorer – we need a modern-day Octavia to get us back on track.

Maxine Peake is a stage, film and television actress.
She has starred in *Dinner Ladies*, *Shameless*, *Silk*
and *The Theory of Everything*.

ISABEL HARDMAN

'I wouldn't like to get into a fight with her,' my teenage self thought the first time I saw a portrait of Octavia Hill. But although she may have looked fierce, she was principled and kind. *The Spectator's* obituary to Hill in 1912 spoke of a life spent 'promoting the best interests of the poor, for whom she cared so well and so wisely', which she did through housing reform.

Yet, she was not a soft touch by any means. Her tales of confrontations with tenants and her emphasis on improving their lives might be considered rather politically incorrect today, and she certainly didn't mince her words:

> *'The difficulty with these people is not financial,*
> *but moral... They must be trained... I say to them,*
> *"You must either do better or you must leave;*
> *which is it to be?"'*

Today, a comment like that would cause fury. But that's the point, isn't it? Because Octavia Hill didn't make those demands of her tenants and leave them alone. She turned up at their door – *her* door actually, for she was the landlady – and then she stuck around, working with those tenants until their behaviour improved. Hill immersed herself in her tenants' lives. Nowadays, landlords often communicate with tenants by email, text or letter, which is efficient when you're managing thousands of homes, but it means that the sort of tenants Hill was referring to are often left to fend for themselves in modern society.

The housing officers I've met express frustration that, often, they have had to place tenants in homes without any hope of long-term contact with them to help them improve their lives. They are only asked to appear when repairs are needed or when disputes require sorting out.

That said, housing associations do run good schemes to help tenants get on in life. But the sheer number of properties and people involved make it very difficult for the modern social landlord to 'improve' tenants in the same way as Hill. She saw herself not just as someone who provided housing, but as someone who provided a way up and out. The policies of successive governments have not helped modern landlords to imitate that model.

Hill worked in a society with a quite different disposition to today's. She would have grieved the extent of state involvement in housing. But she would also have had to adjust to the extent of housing need in London today; Hill's idea of happy homes can only be possible today if there are enough homes available in the first place.

Hill also spoke quite sternly of the obligation of the rich to do what they could to improve the prospects of the poor. However, reforming the housing sector entirely would be a much easier task than enticing some of London's rich to mimic Hill, in an age when developers boast that they have 'no social housing' on site or construct separate entrances for the poor who live in the blocks they build.

In 1912, the leading article in *The Spectator* lamented that social reformers were already forgetting Hill's lessons on poverty. Today, her fierce eyes would be flashing at many others across society who have managed to forget those lessons too.

***

Isabel Hardman is a journalist and associate editor at *The Spectator* magazine.

"I COULDN'T AFFORD
TO LIVE WHERE
I LIVE AND WORK
WHERE I WORK IF
IT WASN'T FOR
SOCIAL HOUSING."

Boyd Emery

THE RT HON. THE LORD BEST

Octavia Hill's aim was 'to make individual life noble, homes happy and family life good', and her efforts set the home in its wider context as the essential foundation for a decent, fulfilling life.

Today, what kind of home will enable its occupants to realise their full potential – as individuals and as families – in the 21st century?

I suggest the answer comes in four parts.

First, we must admit that there are still households living in accommodation almost as squalid and overcrowded as 150 years ago. Acute shortages in so many parts of the UK mean people are homeless or sharing space in conditions that make normal family life impossible. So, just creating enough homes to go round is of primary importance.

Secondly, although it is a pre-requisite, it is not sufficient that we simply increase supply to match demand. The property also has to be affordable. If rents absorb so much income (including the income of those receiving housing benefit where this does not cover all the rent) that there is not enough left for other essentials, then a good life will be impossible. Today's private sector rents, and even so-called 'affordable rents' in social housing, as well as any form of home ownership, are cripplingly expensive in most of the UK for almost everyone under 40. So improving affordability comes a close second.

Thirdly, the characteristics of our properties – design, space, light, warmth, ventilation – make the difference between 'housing' and 'homes'. Octavia Hill would be shocked to learn that this country is building the smallest homes in Europe, miles behind the standards of Scandinavia, Germany and France. We also add insult to injury by 'taxing' poorer households who have a 'spare' room.

Families need space in which to work and play, do homework, have meals together and have friends round. And older people will spend almost all their time within their home: homes need to be light and bright, fully accessible and extremely well-insulated if our lives in retirement are to be comfortable and rewarding.

And, lastly, the Octavia Hill message always went beyond the bricks and mortar: it embraced housing management that treated tenants with dignity and respect; and it recognised the importance of extra opportunities for social interaction and personal development which the provision of housing involves. The great privilege for those – like Octavia Housing – who own and manage thousands of properties is that, in so many ways, they can make those homes the basis for not only freeing people from the miseries of insecure, sub-standard housing but for creating the conditions for lives that are, indeed, noble, happy and good.

But we still have a long way to go.

Lord Best is a member of the House of Lords and a social housing leader. He was President of the Local Government Association from 2005–2015.

TRACEY LOUIS-FERNAND

H aving a home gives you that sense of security that is so important. Yes, a home gives you shelter, a place to sleep and your own private space. But a home also enables you to deal with the really basic things. Any form that you fill in, they'll ask for your name and address. And if you don't have an address, registering with a doctor or a dentist, applying for a job or registering your kids for a school place is almost impossible. You can't move forwards. So many of our day-to-day affairs are connected to our address – on so many levels, where we live is intrinsic to who we are and who we want to be.

Tracey Louis-Fernand is an Acquisitions and New Business Manager in the Development team at Octavia.

CAMPBELL ROBB

M ost people, when asked what's important to them, respond that they value 'homes happy and family life good'. This was Octavia Hill's aspiration 150 years ago. She recognised that decent housing was a central feature to helping to improve people's lives. But how can we fulfil this aspiration today?

At Shelter, we know that a happy home is the foundation to good family life, however, the desperate shortage of secure homes, that are affordable to ordinary families on average incomes, is leading too many people into a downward spiral that ends in homelessness. At the turn of 2015 there were over 90,000 homeless children in England. Having to turn to your local council for help and being placed in a run-down B&B, often miles from your former home, frustrates the very basics of family life: children travelling long distances to school and family meals prepared in a shared kitchen, eaten on laps.

Hill's big concern was the dreadful living conditions of children in Britain's cities, especially London. She found that landlords routinely ignored their obligations to tenants. If she were alive today, I think she would be concerned about the re-emergence of short-term private lettings, which leave families with little bargaining power to address terrible conditions or to challenge exploitative landlords.

Nearly 50 per cent of growth in private renting in the last two years has come from families with children, who now make up nearly a third of private renting households. For such families, a 'forever home' feels like an unattainable dream. Almost half of renters are aged 35+, and nearly a third expect to be renting for the rest of their lives.

A third of privately rented homes do not meet the government's Decent Homes Standard, while almost a fifth contain a health and safety hazard. Shelter research shows that over 60 per cent of renters have experienced problems such as damp, mould, electrical hazards and infestations over the past year, and ten per cent said their health had been affected by housing disrepair in the last year. Further, nine per cent of private-renting parents said their children's health had been affected.

If we're to adequately address today's housing crisis, we can learn a great deal from Hill's response to deplorable housing conditions. Recognising that investment in better properties was the key to delivering good homes, she persuaded wealthy benefactors to invest in social housing. In return for their investment, they received an annuity and once the return was achieved, any surplus was spent on projects such as playgrounds and communal decoration.

Today, a major factor holding back desperately-needed housing development is the availability and cost of land. That's why Shelter advocates New Homes Zones based on a public-private development partnership. Such partnerships allow landowners to invest their assets in exchange for shares in the partnership, or alternatively sell the land to it. Public agencies and private investors, including pension funds and local individuals, are able to invest capital and take a long-term return on their investment, just like Hill's early benefactors.

Hill understood that she had to secure decent homes, let by responsible housing managers, if she was to assist people in living 'noble lives'. This is the approach we must take now to help lift families out of insecurity, poor conditions and homelessness, and ennoble future generations – just as Hill did.

Campbell Robb is the Chief Executive of Shelter, the housing and homelessness charity.

JEAN ROCH

M y dad was born in the East End and my mum was
born in Kilburn. They were both moved to the
Cuckoo Estate in Hanwell which was on the grounds of
the orphanage where Charlie Chaplin went. It was very
forward thinking – beautifully built and everybody had a
garden. They were both brought up there – moved there
from the slums – and they met at the Hammersmith
Palais. My grandfather – my dad's father – was the
youngest of eight and he didn't sleep in a bed until he
went into the army in the First World War! Before that,
he slept on a chair. That was 100 years ago. Not so long
ago really, is it? In my work as a nurse and health visitor,
I've made many home visits over the years and I've seen
some pretty horrendous things in terms of housing. I once
saw a woman and a baby in a property who were sleeping
in a cardboard box.

For me, the opposite of being noble is to be ashamed, and
I think that people who are poor or homeless often feel
ashamed. If you haven't got somewhere to live, how can

you feel noble? If you've got a decent place to live, you don't need to feel ashamed. That's what living a noble life is all about – decency.

Jean Roch is an Octavia resident who lives in Westminster. She is a retired health visitor.

BOYD EMERY

How did you become an Octavia resident?

It's a long story. I hit rock bottom and became homeless 14 years ago. I was an alcoholic and sleeping on the streets around Hammersmith for around seven months. One day I had an epiphany and went to a clinic and said: 'I need help. I need to get off the streets.' After months of trying I got into rehab and spent three months there. There was a specialist project for homeless people at the time and Octavia agreed to take me on.

What was it like to be homeless?

To be honest, it was a relief initially. I'd been struggling to pay rent and I had this bad habit. When I didn't have to struggle to keep things together it was definitely a relief – but that soon wore off. I met people who'd been on the streets for a while; they took me under their wing. Two of us looked after each other. If there's two of you, you're safer. You protect each other, hear about things on the grapevine.

What are your most vivid memories from the time when you were homeless.

Mornings. Feeling sick in the mornings. Feeling cold. People looking at you as though you are nothing. Being treated like something not human. Sometimes I'd get depressed but I did meet people who were very kind. That always allowed me to keep a bit of hope.

What was it like getting a home after your experience of homelessness?

It was a massive thing to get a roof over my head after three years of hostel living. Although hostels are obviously dryer than living on the street, it's not that much different. It felt so good that people wanted – and were able – to help me.

What's your opinion on social housing today?

I feel lucky. I couldn't afford to live where I live and work where I work if it wasn't for social housing. There's a desperate need for it. Building houses only for key workers isn't going to stop the problems – there are lots of people on lower wages than key workers who need to be in London too. There's definitely a need for supporting people as well beyond simply 'here's a house, get on with it'.

Do you have any particular memories associated with the last ten years of living in your home?

I have a lot of memories from the time when I first moved in. I remember sitting there on my new couch looking at the roof over my head and the four walls around me – that really was an amazing feeling! Oh, and when I was moving in, I remember my neighbours saying to me: 'If you need anything, just ask!' I got a really good welcome from my neighbours. I didn't expect to be treated normally because of where I'd come from – but they treated me more than normally, they were… neighbourly.

What does a 'noble life' mean to you?

I think it's about being true to yourself. About being comfortable with who you are. Getting the basics right. If you've got the basics, you can do so much more. That's what Octavia's legacy is all about – she gave people a platform to lead their lives in the way they wanted to.

Boyd Emery is an Octavia resident who has lived in Fulham for around ten years.

JANE BRETHERTON

My husband Michael and I decided to start up a housing association in the sixties when two boys from the local youth club said to Michael: 'Our families are being evicted.' In fact, one of the families had already been evicted by Peter Rachman, who was notorious for his exploitation of tenants. A charity in Norfolk gave us our first £5,000 because they understood about poor housing conditions and people had read all about Rachman by then. The other thing, of course, is that we'd all seen the film *Cathy Come Home* which was absolutely devastating – because of that film, people started to think more about housing problems and about the devastating situations families were living in.

We were frightfully young, only in our twenties, and Michael and I were really enthused and full of energy for the project. We got a team together from the local church and the editor of the *Kensington News* wrote an article which gained us publicity and support. North Kensington is an extraordinary place. It's always been a melting pot and it has got the most amazing atmosphere. We felt as though we were part of that – as though we were part of real life.

We were very conscious of being part of a movement. Setting up a housing association wasn't something we plucked out of the air – it was happening all over London and we had some friends in Battersea who'd done the same thing. They started a housing trust. It was extraordinary to go to dinner parties where people talked about housing trusts – a social movement which was thrilling to be part of. We felt like we were making a difference, especially when the flats we bought were nicely done up and people had central heating and bathrooms – things they'd never had before.

There was an old man who we housed. His name was George, I forget his surname. He had always been homeless but somehow or other he came to us to be housed as a tenant. We sorted him out a bedsit and he was thrilled with it but one day he came to the office and said: 'Could somebody come and help me to learn how to do the hot water?'

It turned out that he'd never used hot water before. 'What did you do about having a bath before?' we asked him. 'Oh, once a month I go to Peckham Market and I buy a new set of clothes and then I go to Waterloo and have a bath. Then I throw my old clothes away and put my new ones on. But I can't do that anymore because they've turned it into mixed bathing. So I need to have a bath in my own bath.' It was quite marvellous really – that sort of thing happened a lot.

Jane Bretherton and her husband **Michael** came to live in North Kensington on their marriage in 1960. They set up the Latimer Housing Society with five other members of St Helen's Church in 1963. The 200 flats owned by Latimer were absorbed by Octavia in 1988.

KAM CHUNG

'Why do people want to live in London when they can't afford it?' I've heard that question asked so many times! It's not about people needing to live in London, it's that London needs those people. What sort of state would London be in if everyone left to live somewhere else? Without our nurses, cleaners, bin men, postal workers, dinner ladies, shop assistants, teachers, doctors, police, firefighters, ambulance crew, plumbers, electricians – the list of workers we rely on every day is almost endless – London would fall to its knees.

That's why we need affordable housing.

Kam Chung is Head of Service Development at Octavia.

ROSALIND

The one thing I feel really passionate about in the wider community is attitudes to people in social housing. I once went for a drink with a guy and he asked me about where I lived. I told him I lived in a housing association property and he said to me: 'What a loser.' It was terrible and it has stayed with me for life. These days, people in social housing are not called 'losers' – rather, people are jealous of seeing others living in central London properties who otherwise couldn't afford it. That sort of attitude does nothing for a cohesive society. It really bothers me quite a lot. Some people have to work two or three jobs just to be able to pay their rent.

Rosalind is an Octavia resident who has lived in Westminster for 35 years. She is semi-retired.

GRETA KENDALL

What Octavia Hill did was a big step for a woman back then. And, she didn't have to do it. I imagine that a lot of people would have said the equivalent of 'yeah, whatever' in those days – but she was determined.

I think we'd use 'self-sufficient' these days instead of 'noble'. It means having security and knowing you don't always have to run around asking for favours or prove yourself to people. I'd been living in private rented accommodation before shared ownership with Octavia and, in a word, it was hideous. Now I'm able to put some roots down. Someone can't just come round and tell you 'you're out in a week'. Having to prove yourself – for example, being asked 'Are you sure you can afford this?' – can be very wearing.

Greta Kendall is a shared owner living in Hounslow.

DAVID ORR

I t is fair to say that we think of ourselves as a civilised and caring nation. Most of us, when we think about it, would say that a key political priority is to ensure that everyone has a decent home. Indeed, so embedded is this idea that we don't think it even needs to be said. And until quite recently, although there were always some who were not properly housed, we could assert, as a nation, that we had come pretty close to meeting that objective.

The perils of complacency. What Octavia Hill was part of starting is now fraying at the edges and is, for many people, in danger of being a distant dream. Her great vision of noble, happy, family life in safe and decent homes has driven so much of our housing thinking in the past 150 years. It has been at the centre of the values and social mission of the housing associations that now provide homes to more than five million people. It is what drove the post-war governments when building millions of homes for ordinary working people. But that recognition of the primary importance of the home to the success of our lives has been eroded. For far too many people, the prospect of a secure, affordable home is out of reach.

How on earth has it come to this? We have the resources, the land, the knowledge and the expertise to build the new homes we need and regenerate those which need new investment. What we have lacked is both political and public will. We prioritise great views and green belt over building the homes people so desperately need. We deny the facts of the housing crisis. We seem to be prepared to allow housing for future generations to be worse than what we have at present. Do we really want to be the first generation to accept a future for our children that is worse than our own present? Could anything be less noble than that?

Octavia Hill saw the problems around her and the terrible conditions people lived in, and made a fuss. She did something about it. She galvanised activity and, as a result, created change that has resonated for 150 years. Those of us who follow in her footsteps have an obligation to think afresh about what changes we want to make – to imagine a future that is better than the present and take steps to deliver that future. To do this means that everyone involved in housing provision must accept the obligation to move beyond service delivery, important though that is. We have to be advocates for those who are voiceless, campaigners against present and future injustice and creators of a better future. That is, indeed, a noble ambition. Our nation's social and economic future depends on us getting this right. Octavia's clarion call to action rings as clearly now as it did 150 years ago.

David Orr is Chief Executive of the National Housing Federation, the umbrella organisation for social housing providers in England.

PAUL MASON

Whenever there's a housing boom, the rich develop the desire to colonise urban space, leaving room, maybe, for a class of servants to co-exist, but squeezing out everybody in between. Octavia Hill's legacy is, even now, the vital physical living spaces built by her movement, and those who followed. But even more important is the ideal she championed – that of mixed communities. As central London gets swallowed up by scarcely-occupied investment homes, while young people sleep two or three to a room just to keep a toehold in the capital, Octavia Hill's mission is not over.

Paul Mason is a journalist and broadcaster. He is Economics Editor at Channel 4 News.

KEITH USHER

have been an Octavia resident since 1986. Getting a property with them couldn't have come at a better time. I had my name down with several housing associations and I was going through a really bad patch. I wasn't on the streets – so homeless is too strong a word – but I was sleeping at a friend's flat. Things weren't wonderful for me at the time. When I got the call and was offered my place I burst into tears. A grown man. I was really pleased – it was so wonderful and I haven't looked back since then.

Private rents are a joke in Kensington and Chelsea and as for the definition of affordable housing... how long is a piece of string? We are going to end up in a situation like Baltimore in the States during the eighties, where all the middle-class people left the centre of the city leaving only the disadvantaged poor. The difference in London will be that the situation will be the other way around – all the service workers will move outside of the centre of London because only the rich can afford to live there.

It's the breakup of the family fabric as well. What happens if you haven't got your gran around the corner to take care of the kids or your mum while you go to work? Childcare is so expensive it's not worth it – earning an income and then spending it all on nursery fees. It's difficult.

Nowadays, it's charitable institutions that are continuing the work of Octavia Hill into the 21st century. When I got my diploma in town planning, my thesis was on the subject of new towns. A lot of the people who set new towns up had a background in religion like Octavia Hill. You might not agree with their religious outlook but there was this sense of doing something noble. I think the word is still good but I think that people can be noble without being religious. Noble, I think, is a fine word, yes, without the religious connotations.

Keith Usher is an Octavia resident who has lived in Ladbroke Grove for 29 years. He is retired.

PETER CLAYTON

There is a plaque to Octavia Hill in Westminster Abbey. One of only three women invited in their own right to Queen Victoria's Jubilee service, the Unknown Woman is now memorialised next to the Unknown Warrior. Later housing managers paid lip service to her methods, but their value was discounted in the resurgence of the caretaker tradition, which tended to focus on buildings. The index of *A History of Social Housing*, published in 1984, excludes her and her grandfather, Doctor Thomas Southwood Smith, 'the father of sanitary reform'. Historians are still inclined to misplace her within the phalanx of middle-class do-gooders for whom slumming was a fashionable activity and self-help the mantra.

Today, her life and work is documented in her Birthplace House in Wisbech, Cambridgeshire. It is not a shrine but an attempt to highlight her family's extraordinary portfolio of achievements. Before there was any government action to ameliorate social conditions and before the local authorities existed, Octavia helped identify the key elements that make 'homes happy and family life good'. They are not that different today. Her authority came from fifty years of managing her communities and facilitating the provision of open spaces, clean air and beauty in all its forms. Her method of close-quarter management was based on a personal knowledge of individuals. This included strong interventions where necessary. It is a template worthy of attention today. The pioneering 1906 twenty-two acre Walworth Estate remains a testament to not just the campaign for but also the delivery of improvements.

She was a public and private advocate for the rights of poor people and a notable fundraiser and networker.

Her vision should surely be our vision. Noble and exemplary lives like hers should still command our attention. Her words to a new management recruit in 1911, the year before she died, resonate across the years:

'I fear I forgot to mention that as we work among a large group holding different religious and political views we have all to be careful to be silent one to another and among the tenants on questions on which we may differ and that I should regret if any of my staff took a public or very pronounced part in political questions. Our work is practical and individual and done best in silence.'

At the core of her work was social inclusion, which remains articulated in the motto of the National Trust: 'Forever, For Everyone'.

Peter Clayton is Chairman of the Octavia Hill Birthplace Museum Trust in Wisbech, Cambridgeshire.

DEBBIE SORKIN

The writer Linda Tirado has described how the condition of being poor – not destitute, but only ever having just enough to get by – colours your whole life. You stop planning for the future and a small change in your circumstances can make an enormous difference to your life. In Linda's words:

> *'It cuts off your long-term brain. It's best not to hope.*
> *You just take what you can get as you spot it.'*

In this position, it can be hard for people to feel noble, or that they deserve dignity and can expect to be treated with respect. People retreat into themselves and don't make the social connections that could enrich their lives.

Many people living in social housing are in this situation. As the *Real London Lives* research project demonstrated, two-thirds of tenants who were able to work were in full- or part-time work. However, 75 per cent of these people were struggling to make ends meet due to low pay, limited working hours and welfare reform. This is part of a broader trend: although unemployment has been falling, there are rising numbers of low-skill jobs, zero-hours contracts and workers being paid below the living wage. And once you're in this position, it can be hard to get out.

In such circumstances, the value of charities and not-for-profit organisations in the social housing sector lies in the work they do to give people back their hope and their dignity, so that they have a better chance of reaching for nobility for themselves and happiness for their families. They help to create options, keep families together and build communities.

The far-reaching work of these organisations would not be possible without the care, empathy and dedication of the individuals who work for them. To give just one example out of many, managers at an Octavia-run day centre went out of their way to provide respite care for an older lady who needed support. Moreover, they replicated the room she was staying in to look like her own flat so that she would feel in familiar surroundings and they also stayed with her to ensure that she was settled and comfortable. In doing all this, they not only helped the lady directly: they also supported her daughter, thereby reducing any potential stress for her.

If Octavia Hill were alive today, she might ask how it has come about that the life chances of so many people in society have been reduced. But she would surely recognise that, around the country, there are numerous people and organisations that share her ambition and – tirelessly and selflessly – work to continue her vision.

Debbie Sorkin is National Director of Systems Leadership at the Leadership Centre and a Board Member of Octavia Housing.

THERESA PALMER

Working as a housing income officer presents a number of challenges. The world has changed since Octavia Hill spoke of making noble lives, happy homes and good family life; the things that could be said and done with a view to supporting people to help themselves and maintain standards back then cannot be said and done today. We have to work within the law. I doubt that Octavia would have tolerated people that did not always pay their rent, but these days our hands are somewhat tied. We don't have much leeway to deal with people who might sometimes take advantage.

That said, it's not just, you know, 'pay us your money, pay us your money' and then we come down hard on them when they don't. Yes, of course, people do need to pay their rent but we are human and understand how tough life can be. It's about trying to encourage people to face up to the situation they're in and offering them help – and I mean realistic, practical help – for example, through welfare and debt advice.

Half the time when people get into these difficult financial situations, the stress they're under means they put the blinkers on and hope that they can resolve the problems themselves, or that their problems will magically disappear. So it's important that we motivate people to seek advice and assistance and – most importantly – to communicate. That's the main thing. Good communication is half the battle; the people I struggle with most are the ones you don't hear anything from, which is a shame because I like to be able to help people wherever I can.

Theresa Palmer is an Alternative Tenures Income Officer administering rent and service charges for Octavia's leasehold properties.

GEORGE LEMOS

'All we are working for is to make individual life noble, homes happy, family life good.' It sounds magnificent; but is it any more appropriate as a precept for the organisation which bears her name today than Octavia Hill's recommendation that 'water should be on every floor but not necessarily in every tenement. It is no hardship for tenants to carry water a few yards on a level passage or balcony'? In this matter, the housing association of the 21st century must surely suppose that it has surpassed more than the plumbing of the 19th century: it would hardly follow Octavia Hill in characterising a group of tenants as an 'ignorant and destructive class of people'. To her successors, a search for the definition of a noble life and its use in judging tenants would seem even more outlandish than trying to let a flat without a bathroom.

As a phrase, 'noble life' is, arguably, obsolete. But in Octavia Hill's time it was common enough and we can, by perusing writers in her milieu, form a good enough idea of what she meant: disregard for the humdrum, a focus on higher things, empathy with others, deep self-reliance and the cultivation of the best in one's individuality.

What has this to do with housing? If you are workless and penniless in a filthy slum, your thoughts are unlikely to rise above anxiety for day-to-day survival. But Octavia Hill was not alone in thinking that fulfilment of our potential must follow the satisfaction of our basic physical needs; the idea can be evidenced in writers as different as Wilde and Keynes.

Keynes's prediction in 1930 that, within a century, economic growth would free us for better things seems quaint. In so-called advanced countries, some still struggle for bare necessities, most have restricted leisure time and almost all consume the leisure time they do have in less than fulfilling ways.

A liberal would say that, being the consequence of individual choice, this outcome cannot be regretted. He would urge the contemporary housing association to remain true to the liberal order in which it is embedded: its professional specialism should be housing standards; in pursuit of efficiency it should mimic the commercial firm; and as a supplier of housing services it should have no more regard to the lives of its customers than a supplier of gas or electricity. An objective and universal standard of human worth, as presumed in the words of Octavia Hill, cannot be acknowledged by liberalism and, even if posited, should not be the business of a utility provider.

And yet: today's housing association may still be a charity and a charity's interests are those of its beneficiaries. The beneficiaries are not just consumers of housing services. Are their lives best improved by the liberal's prescription? Or could it be that liberalism is a deceiving and self-deceiving mask for certain interests that disadvantages others such as the poor? Octavia Hill's invocation of the noble life should make us stop and think.

George Lemos is a financial advisor who has worked with Octavia for many years.

HELEN CONNOLLY

Twenty-three years ago my partner and I came back from working in Spain because he was having a mental breakdown. So I found myself at the age of 62 with a very distressed husband running over Hampstead Heath at four o'clock in the morning or curled up in the corner of people's rooms. We had nowhere to live. One day, a leaflet came through my son's door which said: 'Marylebone Housing Association is opening its list.' I just picked up my coat and decided to go there. My son and partner thought I was crazy: 'You can't just get a housing association property, you need to have four children,' they said. But I went anyway and asked to see the manageress. I told her my problem and after I'd finished she said: 'I can't show you the flat now but could you meet me tomorrow morning?' It was extraordinary. I hugged and hugged her. I have never been so grateful. Later, I guessed that she thought we were a good fit for the two other frail tenants in the house.

In 1992, my road was very rough. Watching the generations become happier and healthier here has been heart-warming and it feels much safer now. There are rich people and struggling people from all over the world. But sadly, many are still isolated and not interacting. I know of people who desperately needed help when they had flu or after an operation and society isn't pulling together. I have experienced this personally as a sufferer of ME. Being part of a housing association has given me security and peace of mind. I'm so grateful and proud to be part of an organisation carrying on Octavia Hill's values.

Helen Connolly is a resident of Octavia who has lived in north Westminster for 23 years. She is a retired youth worker and teacher.

STEVE SMITH

M y parents were born in the 1920s. My Mum lived in a slum in Deptford and Dad lived in a little two-up, two-down cottage on the borders of Greenwich and Lewisham. You know how it was back then. After the war, when they got married, they were eventually given a council flat. They were so elated after the squalor of pre-war housing, even though they had to share rooms with another family. I feel we might be heading back to those days – there just doesn't seem any intent to protect social housing. The term 'social rent' isn't even bandied about any more – it's all about 'affordable housing'. And it's just not that affordable for most people.

The current housing crisis is nothing new. We've had a housing crisis since before I moved out of my mum and dad's house! To be honest, what we've got now is more of a *social* crisis – unfortunately, many of the people who make the decisions have no vested interest in the lives of the people at the bottom. That was what was so pioneering about Octavia's work – her whole ethic was about people and giving them something more than a baseline. If people feel as though they have got a future, they can build on it.

To make the most of Octavia's legacy we've got to go beyond housing, beyond social care and really think about what it is that we need for a fair society. It's not all about money, it's about people – people being happy. Happy families were at the heart of Octavia's ethic. I really think that she was a complete genius.

Steve Smith has lived in Kensington and Chelsea for 26 years. He is a garden designer who won a gold medal at the 2015 RHS Hampton Court Flower Show for his first conceptual garden design on behalf of local mental health charity SMART.

"ALL I NEED FOR A HAPPY HOME IS A KITCHEN, BATHROOM AND TOILET. ONCE YOU'VE GOT THE BASICS, YOU'RE ALRIGHT."

John O'Callaghan

NATALIE BENNETT

W hen I walk around my home community of Somers Town in London, I feel that I can almost put myself in the shoes of Octavia Hill.

Somers Town sits between King's Cross and Euston stations and yet its large, crowded residential community – where, traditionally, poor workers for the railways and associated industries were housed – is little known to the commuters who buzz in and out of those mainline termini.

Nevertheless, it's a rich community in terms of traditional ties and relations: I recall a few years ago being on a protest march on which two locals, by no means regulars at such events, were clearly much more comfortable once they'd established that their grandmothers had been to school together. That strong sense of tradition has been enriched by new arrivals in the community. I think it was in 2010, when canvassing, I happened upon a group of Somali matrons emerging from a coffee afternoon.

I asked if they were voting and, in unison, they pulled from their pockets with a flourish their polling cards: 'Of course,' they said, with passionate intensity.

The flat in which I live, and those of many of my neighbours, aren't quite of the Octavia Hill era – they're mostly 1930s, and of municipal provision of which she wouldn't have approved – but in design and approach they owe much to her pioneering principles. They are good homes – solidly built, thick-walled and designed with an attention to detail that we now seem unable to match. (The original windows in my bathroom, only recently replaced by double-glazing, had extended handles to ensure anyone could reach them from floor level. Their replacements lack this, and I have to climb on the loo to reach them: the risks this presents to older or frailer residents horrifies me.)

As well as being good homes, my flats are arranged around a central quadrangle garden that follows, many decades before their codification, the principles of 'Secured by Design' now espoused by the police.

There's an overarching principle here that standards were to be maintained. And while our modern sentiments don't always agree with old ideas of standards – accounts of families going hungry to buy the lace curtains that my lease still specifies aren't in line with my ideas – the idea that everyone should be able to attain a decent standard of living is one that we desperately need to recapture.

However, in an age in which 'strivers versus skivers' rhetoric has been allowed to run wild, in which the swingeing, random application of benefits sanctions have hit the ill and the disabled with sometimes deadly force, and in which a minimum wage well below that required to maintain basic living standards is accepted as the norm, that claim seems almost to come from another country.

So, I think we have much to learn from Octavia Hill's 'noble life' – standing up for the principle that a decent home should be available for *everyone*, as part of a secure life, lived without fear of want in warm, comfortable surroundings.

Natalie Bennett has been leader of the Green Party of England and Wales since September 2012.

PROFESSOR PAUL DOLAN

When I was asked by the Office for National Statistics (ONS) to help them in their objective to measure the nation's happiness, I knew we'd need to pose more than one question. In addition to asking people how happy they feel, I believed it was also important to ask about how worthwhile their activities are. Noble individual lives, happy homes and good family lives do not just reflect happiness and pleasure. It is important to balance fun activities, like watching television, with worthwhile and fulfilling activities, like taking care of other people. Although everyone needs a different balance of each in order to be truly happy, we all need at least some pleasure and some purpose.

Homes are important for happiness, primarily because of the time we spend inside them. Whilst many people aspire to own their own homes, or to own a large home, what is more important for our happiness is what happens inside the four walls. Overall, the circumstances of life, like income or the number of cars in the garage, matter much less for happiness than how we spend our time and whom we spend it with. The happiest homes are filled with people who spend their time doing activities that they find fun and fulfilling.

And so, noble individual lives, happy homes and good family lives are best characterised by the activities and people that are part of these things, rather than by the postcode in which they reside. Homes can, and should, be designed to make happy people and activities more likely. Behavioural science teaches us that most of what we do is not so much thought about, it simply comes about. Whether or not you buy a bar of chocolate depends largely on whether or not it is on display at the till. If you want to spend more time talking and less time watching TV, then set up the TV in a spare room instead of in the kitchen or living room. If you want to encourage reading, leave a variety of books and magazines in communal spaces. Even fresh scents make people more likely to clean up after themselves. Happiness can be achieved by design.

Professor Paul Dolan is an internationally-renowned expert on happiness, behaviour and public policy. He is currently a Professor of Behavioural Science at the London School of Economics. His book *Happiness by Design* was published in 2014.

SASKIA DAKIN

If you don't have a happy home then you are not going to be a very happy person. You probably won't do well in school, work, or in life generally. You won't want to be with anyone if your home isn't nice. Everything is going to be bad.

What do you think you need for a happy home?

A nice mum.

That's important.

And plug sockets…for your mobile phone chargers.

When you think about your home here, what sort of things come to mind? When you're at school and it gets to 2pm and you want to go home, what are the things that you are thinking about?

My bed and pasta and my mum and my brother and my laptop. I don't really know… a nice hot shower. Just sitting on the sofa, relaxing, and just being comfortable, not having to worry about other people.

What would it mean to you if you didn't have your home for whatever reason? It won't happen, but if you didn't have your home, if you lost your home, how would you feel?

I'd feel sad, because then I won't have everything that I take for granted and I wouldn't have any plug sockets.

That's important.

It is very important. If I didn't have this home and if I was worse off, I don't really know what it would feel like because right now I have everything that I need.

Saskia Dakin is a 16-year-old Octavia resident living with her mother and brother in Fulham.

SIR BERT MASSIE

When I was a trustee of a housing association I learned not to talk about houses, flats, apartments or bungalows but to refer, instead, to dwellings. I prefer to use the word homes. Homes are places of security, comfort and the base from which we make our contribution to the world. Or at least they should be. But whatever we call it, a home is usually a building.

What do I expect of a home? Location is important but a home should be well built and designed to meet the demands of modern life. It must be sufficiently large. Some modern housing appears to have been designed for successful clients of Weight Watchers, as the rooms are so small. A home needs to meet not just the demands of the first buyer or occupant but of the many people who will call it home before it is demolished.

But most housing or homes are not suitable for me because I cannot get into them and, if I can, I find I can move no further than the first room I enter. No, I am not a monster but I do use a wheelchair. I am hardly unique. There are approximately 1.2 million wheelchair users in the UK and many people who are fit and healthy now will need a wheelchair at some point in the future. That is when they will find that the place they call home was not designed with wheelchair users in mind.

It need not be this way. Habinteg Housing Association, and others, worked for many years to develop Lifetime Homes and wheelchair housing. Although housing designed specifically for wheelchair users will always form the minority of total housing stock, there is no reason why every new home should not be designed to Lifetime Homes standards. These standards require access and design features of immediate value, such as higher plug sockets, that are easier to reach and help prevent falls. Other features enable the home to be adapted later so, for example, a through the floor lift could be fitted. These features would add just £521 to the cost of building the home. If the home lasts 70 years, that is equivalent to £7.44 a year or 14 pence a week. Compare this with the £273 it costs for an extra night in hospital or £550 a week for residential care, often needed because a disabled person cannot return to their inaccessible home.

Just before the 2015 election, the government introduced a new standard that meets many of the basic access requirements but does not make them mandatory and relies on local planning authorities to apply them. Builders are able to appeal against them. It is understandable that house builders want to build as cheaply as possible and resist anything that adds costs. However, the short-term savings will result in higher costs later and significant inconvenience for occupants. As a society, we should be building homes that all of us can use – not just the fit and strong.

Disabled people can, and do, lead noble lives but it is easier to do so from the base of a noble home: an accessible home.

Sir Bert Massie is a disability rights campaigner. During the last 40 years he has been involved with over 30 disability organisations. He was Chair of the Disability Rights Commission from 2000–2007.

RITA SHALOM

used to live with my mum and dad but then I became disabled. They couldn't accommodate me, so I had to move out. I got burgled at my last place and I needed to move on. I've been living in my current home for about 19 years now. The location is ideal – my husband can commute to work, I can take the children to school, I'm close to my parents and there are good local amenities. I can use my electric wheelchair to get out and about. But most of all, the layout of my house is ideal for someone who's disabled. It's important to be able to access things like my wheelchair and my medical stuff as well as things for the children – the cot, the toys etc.

Things aren't always easy. I couldn't charge my electric wheelchair without someone to help me. I store it in the toilet because I can't house it outside. But it's good to live in a space that isn't just for disabled people. I don't feel like an outsider. Living in a home with only disabled people doesn't seem right – we're all 'normal' – it's just nice to live in a community. When my children were in full-time education, I wanted to get back into doing something worthwhile. I didn't want to waste my life away at home; I have skills that I wanted to put to use. I knew that Octavia ran an employment service so I got in contact. A voluntary position came up in the Estate Services team and so I did some work for them. It was daunting at first! You might know your way around your home computer but when you are out there in the workplace, it's different.

But it was nice to wake up with a purpose other than to look after myself and my family. I really enjoyed not being at home. I did that job for two days a week, for several months. Since then I've been doing voluntary work at my children's school.

Being part of a community is like having a second family. I see people hanging up their washing, parking their cars. People you learn to trust, who can trust you. It's quite a mixed community. We all look out for each other.

You don't need to be of high class or high rank to live a decent life. People adapt to what they have and I think that these days people are quite happy to have a roof over their heads. A noble life is all about having privileges, right? I think that still stands. It's a privilege for me to be here. I wouldn't change it.

Rita Shalom is an Octavia resident. She has lived in a property in Brent for nearly 20 years.

ALAIN DE BOTTON

Our sensitivity to our surroundings can be traced back to an enigmatic feature of human psychology: the way we harbour within us many different selves. Not all of these personas feel equally like 'us', so much so that in certain moods – or at certain times – we may experience a sense of having come adrift from what we judge to be our 'true' selves.

Unfortunately, the self we yearn for at such moments – the elusively authentic, creative and spontaneous side of our character – is not ours to summon at will. Our access to it is, to a humbling extent, determined by the places we happen to be in, by the colour of the bricks, the height of the ceilings and the layout of the streets. In a house strangled by motorways, or in a wasteland of rundown tower blocks, our optimism and sense of purpose risk being drained away, like water from a punctured container. In uncomfortable or unedifying surroundings, we may start to forget that we ever had ambitions or reasons to feel spirited, hopeful and happy.

Indirectly, all of us depend on our surroundings to embody the moods and ideas we respect and cherish, and to remind us of them. We feel comforted if the buildings in which we work and live reflect who we are or who we want to be. We arrange around us material forms which communicate to us what we need – but are at constant risk of forgetting what we need – within. We turn to wallpaper, benches, paintings and streets to staunch the disappearance of our true selves.

In turn, those places whose outlook matches and legitimates our own, we tend to honour with the term 'home'. Our homes do not have to offer us permanent occupancy or store our clothes to be worthy of the name. To speak of home in relation to a building is simply to recognise its harmony with the things we believe are most important. As the French writer Stendhal put it: 'What we find beautiful is the promise of happiness.'

What we call a beautiful home is one that helps to restore or maintain our equilibrium and which encourages emotions of which we are in danger of losing sight. For example, an anxious person may be calmed by an empty, white, minimalist house. Or a business executive who spends her life shuttling between airports and steel and glass conference centres may feel an intense attraction to a simple rustic cottage – which can put her in touch with facets of her personality that are sidelined during the busy working day. We call something beautiful whenever we detect that it contains, in a concentrated form, those qualities in which we personally – or our societies more generally – are deficient. We respect a style that can move us away from what we fear and towards what we crave: a style which carries the correct dosage of our missing virtues.

Alain de Botton is a philosopher, broadcaster and writer. He has written on love, travel, architecture and literature and in a TED talk seen by nearly four million people, he has called for 'a kinder, gentler philosophy of success'. His books have been bestsellers in 30 countries.

PROFESSOR DUNCAN MACLENNAN
AND DR JULIE MIAO

Economists, whilst recognising the importance of home and community, have well-developed definitions of what constitutes housing and neighbourhood. Housing is seen as a geographically fixed, durable asset with multiple attributes or characteristics. These attributes are used in conjunction with household time and other resources to generate streams of different 'housing services'.

These different housing services contribute to a range of key activities that influence the wellbeing of individuals and households. Typically, the physical characteristics of a dwelling – including its design, size, layout and internal amenities – provide shelter, privacy and comfort (or lack thereof). Emphasis on these physical attributes of homes is still at the forefront of housing policy assessments of housing needs, and although they are essential and relatively easy to identify, they fail to take account of other housing attributes that might reflect or reinforce poverty. Regarding housing and housing policy as primarily about shelter is not enough.

Housing and neighbourhood choices are immutably joined, so that choosing a home sets a household in the context of the private amenities, public services, physical environments and social networks that revolve around the dwelling. A home provides the opportunity for strong and weak connections with neighbours and it influences the time and money that household members expend to connect the different, often widespread, locations at which they pursue different work, leisure and consumption activities with different people. For most households the home is the key focus of social and spatial connections and networks. In this millennium, housing policies have been more carefully constructed within neighbourhood and locational settings, in acknowledgement of some of the drivers of poverty that Octavia Hill and Joseph Rowntree recognised long ago.

Other connections have come to play an increasing role in the ways in which homes are used. Connections over time, as well as space, matter. Memories play a key role in shaping houses into homes. Past housing choices influence current housing choices. Expectations regarding future house prices play a key role in housing decisions as home-ownership has come to constitute the major source of both wealth and debt for many people in a number of advanced economies. And looking to the future, home – that quintessential haven of privacy – is increasingly becoming a wired hub for household activities that spread well beyond the neighbourhood into the global. Emerging homes with energy and movement sensors will increasingly shape energy use and the delivery of care and health support for elderly populations. Faster and better internet access, embedded in the physical structures of the home, will place the household in a home surrounded by a world of accessible information and connectedness to global social and economic networks. Increasingly, the home will become a place to learn and work as well as rest and play. Connection, as much as shelter and location, should lie at the core of better housing for the poor and it will increasingly drive future housing policies and perceptions of what constitutes adequate housing.

Professor Duncan Maclennan is an international expert on the development of neighbourhoods and cities. He is currently Director of the Centre for Housing Research at the University of St Andrews. **Dr Julie Miao** joined the same centre as a Research Fellow in January 2013.

"A NOBLE LIFE IS ABOUT PAYING BACK WHAT YOU GOT OUT OF LIFE. YOU'VE GOT TO GET THE BALANCE RIGHT BETWEEN GIVING AND TAKING. IF YOU LEAVE IT TOO LONG, YOU'LL POP YOUR CLOGS AND YOU WANT TO BE ABLE TO GET TO THE PEARLY GATES AND SAY 'RIGHT, I'M READY NOW LADS!'"

Dennis Flavin

BERYL STEEDEN

I t was one of those memorable light bulb moments in life when an email arrived from my colleague Dr Ann Wilcock, who had been commissioned to write a scholarly history of occupational therapy by the British Association and College of Occupational Therapists. We had already been collaborating for some time on the research when Ann sent me this excited email in which she explained that recurring references to Octavia Hill in the material she had been reading had uncovered the influence that Hill had had on the development of the profession through her relationship with Dr Elizabeth Casson, founder of the UK's first school of occupational therapy in 1930.

This sent me on a fascinating journey to help fill in the gaps in the story. I discovered that there was an Octavia Hill Society and a Birthplace House Museum in Wisbech, set up largely due to the energies of Peter Clayton. A phone call with Peter brought the revelation that, as I sat talking to him from my office in Borough High Street, London SE1, I was looking out over Octavia's Red Cross

Hall and Cottages, where Elizabeth Casson had worked for Octavia as secretary from 1908–13.

Whilst working at Red Cross, Elizabeth was able to use her creative talents and contacts, organising plays and concerts amongst the many activities associated with Octavia's belief in people, well-housed, with access to the 'green sitting room' of outside space, public art and participation in healthy pursuits. The experience of this model in some of the poorest areas in London helped determine Elizabeth's next course of action to qualify as a doctor, the first woman to do so from Bristol University and to specialise in psychiatry, winning the prestigious Gaskell prize in 1927. Her experiences led her to believe in the value of occupation as a curative medium and this took her to the United States, where occupational therapy was named as a profession in 1917.

Today, over 35,000 occupational therapists in the UK apply this understanding in hospital, educational, prison, residential, community and many other settings, as well as in academia.

Beryl Steeden is the Head of Membership and External Affairs at the College of Occupational Therapists.

ALEX FOX

As we receive a continuous drip feed of stories about queues outside hospital A&E departments, abuse scandals and failures in care homes and other institutions, the idea of helping vulnerable adults achieve 'a noble life' through care and support can seem unrealistic. Surely care and support for these members of our society first needs to be safe, reliable and timely, before it is realistic to aspire for anything more 'noble'?

Hill hoped her public service would make 'lives noble, homes happy and family life good'. These are aspirations which are both ambitious and simple. They describe not some luxury, idealised service, but the foundations of a good life and as we can see in today's health and care services, it is in fact only by aiming for a good life that we can achieve the basics of safety, quality and consistency of care and support.

As we have seen all too frequently in the news, people who use care services are often most at risk when they are reliant for their safety and basic dignity on people paid to be with them for brief, pressurised shifts. We cannot aim only for the most basic levels of care and expect to find vulnerable people living their lives safely, let alone happily. The goal must remain, 'lives noble, homes happy and family life good'.

Alex Fox is Chief Executive of Shared Lives Plus, a UK charity providing family-based and small-scale care and support to older and disabled people. He has been named one of Britain's New Radicals by NESTA, in partnership with *The Observer*.

CONCEIÇÃO MELO

I worked in care but I was on a zero-hours contract, which was very unpredictable. I never knew what my income would be and, sometimes, the cost of getting to a job made it impossible – I couldn't afford the bus fares. I ran up huge debts despite working long hours. It was so stressful.

I have four children – three boys aged 22, 24 and 29 and a daughter, Bruna, who passed away at the age of 19 in 2011. She never walked or talked but she was beautiful. We cared for her at home and Octavia helped us to put equipment in the house so I could look after her.

When she died it was very hard. I was depressed and things got on top of me – I had rent arrears and a £2,000 water bill. When I couldn't pay the rent, Octavia contacted me – it made me realise that I had to speak to someone. I used to be really close to Mr Osei, my neighbourhood officer. I told him everything and he was fantastic but at the time my daughter died I had a different neighbourhood officer and I couldn't open up to someone new. However, when the arrears letter came, I knew I had to get some help.

I met with Niki, a Financial Inclusion Officer. She went through my outgoings and told me that, on my current income, I would never be able to afford my rent. Niki saved my life.

I had no money for food. She offered me some food vouchers but you feel shame. I didn't want to use vouchers.

First, she put me in touch with the Citizens Advice debt service. Then she arranged for a grant for my water bill; now, instead of £2,000, I owe £400 and I am paying it in manageable instalments.

We also talked about my care experience and Niki recommended me to one of her colleagues who helps people to find jobs and training. Shortly after I was contacted about a job opportunity in one of Octavia's care homes.

I was invited to come in for an interview. But on the day, I got to the office then turned around and left. I was too nervous. I just stood outside and cried. What could I do – go home and tell my kids I had run away?

Thank goodness I went back in for the interview. I didn't have a lot of confidence and I had to ask the interviewer to repeat things... but I got the job!

Soon, a permanent position came up and my manager suggested I apply. The confidence I had gained in a few months was enormous. The second interview was much easier – and, again, I got the job!

So much stress has been lifted from my shoulders and I am so grateful.

When I think back to how scared I was at the first interview, I wanted to turn and run. But I needed my kids to know that life does get better and you have to stick at things. My eldest son is studying to be a nurse – I think that's because he helped me to care for his sister. For the first time since my daughter passed away I feel a sense of achievement and that things are finally going in the right direction.

Conceição has been an Octavia resident since 2006. She lives in Willesden and works as a Care Assistant for Octavia.

DIANE PHILLIPS

I am really pleased that I work as a day centre manager because it is all about helping people. There are some people here whose dementia level is very high. You can ask them a question but you wouldn't get an answer – that's what dementia is like. There's a lady who comes here from outside the borough – a Jamaican lady. She's very young, only 64, and can't string a sentence together, bless her. Our breakthrough with her came one day when I asked her if she liked Carnival and her eyes flickered and I thought: 'Ooh!' I asked her if she liked Bob Marley or Desmond Dekker but I didn't get a response. So I started singing a Desmond Dekker number and all the other people at the day centre joined in – they knew the song from their younger days. As we sang, the lady took my hands and started dancing, and that was our breakthrough – through music. Now, she looks at people and smiles. She's got a beautiful smile and, sometimes, as she smiles she might put a hand on your cheek.

It's hard to put into words how my work makes me feel – it makes me happy but it can make you feel really sad as well. You don't want a pat on the back for your efforts but it's important to know everything you've done for people is worth it, because it could be *your* parent who needs help one day. Or yourself. That lady with dementia who's only 64 – that could be me one day. I've just turned 60.

Diane Phillips is the Manager of The Quest, a day centre in Notting Hill for older people with dementia or mental health needs.

ALICE CAFFYN

Having a noble life is about helping to develop a sense of community. It means being there for people. Not necessarily for life or death matters – to an outsider it might not look like very much. It's just being there for someone to talk to or for someone to confide in.

Through befriending sessions, vulnerable or isolated members of society can really feel part of their local community, that they are not alone. I've really enjoyed befriending people in my community. I did it for a long time because it is so rewarding. After a while I didn't feel as though I was volunteering – it became part of my everyday life.

Recently, I was a befriender for a gentleman named Joachim. Joachim doesn't have any family in the UK and the family he does have in Germany and Poland are not in contact with him much. In many ways, I was like a replacement family member to him. If a week went by and I hadn't seen him – over Christmas, for example – the first thing he'd say to me when I saw him was: 'Oh, I missed you so much.' For Joachim, my visits were about breaking up his routine, giving him some stability and someone to rely on.

Befriending Joachim was a lot easier than I expected. He is a very friendly, outgoing person. We come from very different backgrounds, our educational experiences are not alike and he's had quite a hard life – I thought the chemistry might not be there at first, but actually it came very naturally. My sessions with him have definitely changed the way I think. I don't make assumptions and seeing how other people live their lives and interact with their neighbours has been an eye-opener.

Being there for Joachim was quite a lot of responsibility actually and it's not something that professional services can provide. I'm not isolated and I have family around me so sometimes that makes me feel a bit guilty. Many people, like Joachim, are not in such a privileged position. It's a privilege having a happy home. In fact, very few people have that.

I think that contributing to your community and giving your time really encapsulates that idea of a noble life – a human connection.

Alice Caffyn volunteered with the Octavia Foundation as a befriender for one-and-a-half years. She works for the Japan Society, an educational charity and membership organisation.

MARTHA MORAN

For people in residential care, life is more than just getting up in the morning and having your basic needs met; it's the whole package – your social needs, your wellbeing, your family commitments, your role within the community. Actually, it's even more than that. It's about giving them the support to achieve their dreams, or some of them at least. If there is something my residents would like to do and we can facilitate it – and it's not too dangerous! – then, obviously, we'll go for it. They might want to go to a party. So we'll take them to a party. But if they want to go on the London Eye, another member of staff will need to take them because I'm not going up there!

But on a more fundamental level, it is important that people in residential care are empowered to do things for themselves, even if someone else can do them more quickly. I once walked into a care home and there was one member of staff going around brushing all the residents' hair. I thought to myself: 'What's going on? Why are you brushing people's hair using the same hairbrush? Why is people's dignity not being preserved?' If someone can brush their own hair, let them brush their own hair, even if it takes them longer than you brushing it. It's their hair.

It means so much to me to see people well cared for, valued, looked after, enabled and to feel as though they are part of something. I would like to think that, one day, if I am in the same situation, I will have that sort of care.

Martha Moran is the Scheme Manager at Park Lodge, an extra care scheme in Hounslow offering 36 residents their own homes with 24-hour care and support.

EVA MILLS

remember once when a bomb dropped on our flat. They'd tried to get the electricity board that was nearby but they missed it and got our flat instead. We never moved out though. I was born in 1937 so I was only young at the time. I don't recall being frightened. We all just mucked in together.

Having a noble life means being able to do things for yourself. Like reading – I can't read letters and that sort of thing, even with a magnifying glass. Or doing the housework – opening boxes and cartons. My life has changed since I lost my sight. To be able to do things yourself – that's nice. When you've always been able to do something and you no longer can, and you have to ask people to do things for you, it's difficult. I suppose it's because of pride. I feel bad that I can't read to my great-grandchildren.

Eva Mills is an Octavia resident who has always lived in the St John's Wood area. Now retired, she previously worked as a cleaner and telephonist.

MOHAMMED GBADAMOSI

Providing help with day-to-day tasks doesn't only have a positive impact on our residents; their families benefit too. There was one particular lady who moved in here – for years her daughter had not been able to go away for fear that she couldn't leave her mum by herself. The daughter thought that if she took a holiday or went away for a few days, there would be no one to support her mum if she needed help. Since the lady has been living here, the daughter has been able to go on two holidays – within three months! It meant a lot to her to know that she could go away from time to time, safe in the knowledge that her mum was well looked after.

There was also something that happened during Christmas when the daughter came to collect this lady for the Christmas break. I'd had a baby about two months before, and when this lady was leaving, she gave me a hug and said: 'That hug is not for you, it's for the baby.' The daughter couldn't believe that her mother could remember what happened two months ago. She was almost in tears.

Some of our residents have lost touch with relatives over the years and so the closest they've got to family is probably the staff here. When our residents pass away, we make it a priority to attend their funerals – not because they've been here, gone and that's the end of it – we attend their funerals because it is important to us to pay our last respects. When people come in here, they become part of us – part of the James Hill House family.

Mohammed Gbadamosi is the Manager at James Hill House, an extra care scheme in North Kensington offering homes for 30 older people with mental and physical health needs. Mohammed was recently named Best Home Care Manager in London in the 2014 Great British Care Awards.

RICHARD MULLENDER

n my view, a noble person is somebody who does something for a common cause. It's about doing something in a way that makes other people's lives better. Noble people may want to get something out of making other people's lives better but, essentially, their focus is the impact they have on other people.

A noble person is acutely aware of how their actions affect other people and always seeks to make sure that those actions have the best impact rather than the worst. They act for the common good.

To be noble, you've got to be the sort of person who sees life beyond yourself. That's not to say that such people don't enjoy their lives, that they don't get annoyed or that they don't feel or act selfishly sometimes – but whenever they do something, they do it with concern for others' welfare. A noble person could be compared to someone with power or responsibility who looks after everyone else, such as a headteacher or hospital ward manager – they don't just look after themselves and their own interests. I love meeting people who look after others and do things for strangers without any sense of taking anything from it. I'm sure they do get something from it – everyone gets something – but the crucial point is that they are not fundamentally self-serving.

A significant part of my role as a hostage negotiator involved listening. Listening, not hearing. The ability to listen is ennobling as it lets the person talking to you know that they have a voice and that you will listen carefully to what they are going to say; that you acknowledge that you are no better than they are and that what they've got to say is extremely important. You may not believe in the same things. That's of no relevance. It's about respect. If I am looking to persuade someone to take a particular course of action, it is ennobling that the person I'm talking to is not made to feel that they are wrong. Who knows what's happened in their life or what values they've picked up along the way? The moment you tell someone 'You're wrong' strips them of their life story. The moment you do that means that you alienate the person you are talking to.

You can't stand in someone else's shoes but what you can do is uncover their values, their beliefs, their crises – all the things that make them tick. If you are going to persuade anybody to do something, you have got to persuade them through them, not through you. A lot of people have been through tough lives and it is important not to be judgemental.

Richard Mullender is a former hostage negotiator and lead trainer at the National Crisis & Hostage Negotiation Unit at Scotland Yard. He is now a full-time speaker and trainer.

LESLIE BRETT

Through the befriending scheme I met Estelle. She likes going to the theatre. She once got me David Essex's autograph – I thought that was really nice. When I met her for the first time I realised that we got on well and before I left that day we agreed 'Every Tuesday, at 11 o'clock' – and that was it. So, Tuesdays have become my volunteering day. One week, Estelle rang me up and said to me: 'I don't need much this week, maybe there is something else you'd like to do?' I replied: 'No, sorry Estelle, Tuesday is *your* day!' The moment I met Estelle I thought: 'That's it, no matter what else goes on in my life, Tuesday is Estelle's day.'

I've always liked saying hello, talking to people. Even when I was a young child I used to get to know the workmen digging up the roads. The first time I made some cakes I gave them a couple and they'd ask me to play them a tune on my recorder. It's important to be understanding, to understand what's happening around you.

With Estelle I listen. We talk. We talk a lot. We never stop talking to be honest. I really like talking to Estelle and we have some nice conversations. Being there for her makes me feel good about myself. When someone lets you into their home there is a build up of trust and empathy too, which I think is very important. It's about being there and taking time.

My relationship with Estelle works both ways. It gets me out of the house every Tuesday and it's something separate; it's completely different to helping out my aunty or one of my other relations. With Estelle, I am maybe more committed because she relies on me to come every week. For something like that to work, it begins with the C-word – Commitment.

Leslie has been a befriender with the Octavia Foundation since March 2014. He has always lived in North Kensington. Leslie is retired but loves music and playing the drums, guitar, harmonica and ukulele.

"MAN IS NOT A SOLITARY ANIMAL. PEOPLE ARE SOCIAL AND THEY NEED A COMMUNITY."

Lina Clifford

DR ELIZABETH BAIGENT

'I have a strong belief that…we have made great mistakes from believing that we have to manage and direct the poor.…we have mainly to take care to remove all obstacles to their living nobly.'

T hus wrote the young Octavia Hill, and she expanded her views on nobility in 1884. She identified 'two primary blessings, the power of entering into divine and human love', and argued that 'we all possess [these primary blessings] – high and low, rich and poor'. Then there were 'secondary gifts – music, colour, art, nature, space, quiet' – but, she exclaimed, 'how unequally these [secondary gifts] are divided'. Rich people had the lion's share of the secondary gifts, she thought, not because they were inherently nobler or better able to enjoy them, but because of their greater wealth and education.

Hill did not campaign for wealth equality, but sought to bring the ennobling secondary gifts of music, colour, art, nature, space and quiet to poor people. She arranged concerts and art shows for them, decorated and brought flowers into the places where they lived, and opened gardens and wilder open spaces to them. Several contemporaries undertook similar reforms, and all were praised, caricatured and criticised. Were flowers or paintings really what poor people needed? Were the reformers really trying to make poor people tractable rather than noble? The efficacy of and motivation behind ennobling projects were questionable, but reformers like Hill sincerely believed that everyone could appreciate the 'nobler' things in life, and that these things were important.

As a Christian, Hill believed that ennobling music, colour, art, nature, space and quiet were 'secondary *gifts*', given by God to humanity, so that those who had them in abundance had a duty to share them – something which would ennoble givers and receivers. Gifts of money or goods, by contrast, reduced poor recipients to ignoble dependency and permitted rich donors ignobly to salve their consciences while keeping the poor at a distance.

Because of her particular vision of nobility, Hill toiled to bring order, self respect, aspiration, and enjoyment of music, art and nature to poor people, at the same time as campaigning against much private charity and public welfare. Hill's vision was not of a country built on the noble aspiration that all should be free from want, but of individual lives lived nobly regardless of class.

Despite the idealism of the quotation which starts this piece, Hill insisted on 'managing and directing' the poor to prevent their acting ignobly. Her middle-class lady 'fellow-workers' closely supervised her tenants to make sure their money was spent on the rent, not in the pub. Her middle-class colleagues of the Charity Organisation Society minutely investigated applicants for charity to make sure they were 'deserving' and not 'spongers'. However, she also undertook 'removing obstacles' so that poor people could enjoy the nobler things in life – often independent of richer people. She taught her tenants to sing and play the violin, grow flowers, produce their own artworks and get out into nature by themselves, and she celebrated their small contributions to her open space fundraising.

Hill's work, then, centred around her ideas of a noble life and her reforms were premised on the need for 'nobler imaginings' of life, and the need for 'mightier struggles' to bring that nobility within reach.

Dr Elizabeth Baigent is a Reader in the History of Geography at the University of Oxford. She is the author of *Nobler imaginings and mightier struggles: Octavia Hill, social activism and the remaking of British society* (2014).

CHARLIE PHILLIPS

You grew up in Notting Hill in the sixties after arriving in London from Jamaica. What was it like back then?

The area was always considered to be a ghetto. When I say 'ghetto', I mean that a lot of the buildings were burnt out and properties had been condemned. In the sixties, parts of the neighbourhood were a 'no-go' area. But a lot of immigrants – Irish, Hungarian, Afro-Caribbean – settled in the area because it was cheap and also because there was plenty of employment from companies such as Lyons, Lucozade, Beechams and Wall's Ice Cream. There were also a lot of cottage industries – dressmakers, dry-cleaners etc. – which gave economic stability and opportunity to the immigrant community.

What memories do you have of growing up in that part of London?

Both happy and sad. There was a lot of racial tension at that time, rioting, Teddy Boys attacking black communities…

and I have flashbacks of Oswald Moseley giving his speeches. As a kid, I remember having to be in by 9pm because of fear of race attacks. But socially, it was a very rich environment and the community was very tight-knit. I can remember, when I was older, waiting outside the pub and someone would bring me a shandy. We'd listen to rhythm and blues music in after-hours 'shubeens' and create our own entertainment. The Piss House Pub was an unofficial community centre in the area back in the sixties and seventies. It was a meeting place for different people – black and white, Caribbean and Irish. Colour wasn't an issue and we were all from the same class – we were all working-class people. My experiences growing up in the area informed my photography. When I was young I never entertained the idea of becoming a serious photographer or documenter of my community, however, photography opened up my imagination. That's how it all started for me. Over time, I wanted to document all aspects of the neighbourhood where I grew up and the Piss House Pub was an important part of that.

How has the area changed?

Over the years, many working-class people have been driven out due to high property prices, speculators and social and economic deprivation. There are no more affordable pubs for working-class people and cottage industries and small businesses have been converted into flats. When I was growing up, we had a strong community spirit. And a strong sense of community creates self-respect, self-sufficiency and greater independence. This spirit has gone from Notting Hill and the area now seems like a clone of so many other places.

How can we get back that sense of community?

It's important to have dignity in life. And to live a dignified life you need a strong community in which people come together but who don't forget about their cultural background. If we are to bring that sense of community back we need better housing, better economic conditions and better social services. But most of all we need stronger networking between all groups in society.

Charlie Phillips has been described in *Time Out* as 'the greatest London photographer you've never heard of'. Jamaican-born, his photographs of everyday life in Notting Hill in the 1960s and 1970s have been shown at Tate Britain, the V&A and the Museum of London.

EILEEN CRAWFORD

I have lived in the same square all my life, around Salsbury Street. When we were little, growing up, it was like a village. Isn't it nice to walk around somewhere knowing that everyone knows you? Everyone knew each other back then; nobody shut their doors. There was a club called the Four Feathers which had a little dance place – everyone used to go there. We went to the Regal for Saturday morning pictures. People never wanted to move out because it was such a great community. We used to have to keep our own front step clean and chop wood on the balcony because there was no heating then. It was spotless and people took ever so much pride in their homes. We took pride in scrubbing the steps and windowsills. We used to be called Marylebonites but there are not very many of us left.

We are losing our identity now and it's because our young people are not being housed. They can get a job but it's so easy down the line to be made redundant. For younger people, it's like they are living in limbo – a two-year tenancy here, a two-year tenancy there. And what about all the young people who cannot get housed at all? I feel very sad for the children growing up around here. They won't have the same sense of community, the same feelings that I had, the same sense of pride we had in the way we lived.

I think Octavia was a marvellous woman because she didn't have to do the work she did. For someone like her to put her time into helping other people, what a wonderful nature she must have had. It's her we've got to thank for the fact that we've got trees in Marylebone Road, you know. What a wonderful woman she must have been. Such compassion, humanity and consideration. How many people nowadays are like that, can you honestly say? If people at the top nowadays actually bothered to look at how people are living, they might get an insight.

It's very easy to fall into a trap of just thinking about yourself. But that's not the right way to live. You've got to have consideration for the people around you. There's a lot of very lonely old people out there.

Eileen Crawford has lived in Marylebone all her life. She is the third generation of her family to live there.

GABRIELLE TIERNEY

think the term 'equal opportunities' went out of fashion about two decades ago but I never forget how important *equality* of opportunities and *access* to opportunities still are in society. I really do feel like the tables are tilted in life in that some people start life in a very privileged position and others don't. In my view, a key part of the work we do is to be a broker of opportunities in order to make the playing field a little bit more level for people. Sadly, the changing landscape of social welfare is having a negative impact on a lot of people, especially those who are on low incomes, who are disabled or who are elderly. There are plenty of people out there who aren't in a privileged position but who have impressive skills and a lot to offer their local communities. By giving them the means to harness that opportunity, their lives can be transformed.

Art, for example, is really powerful for a lot of groups we work with. While economics or politics might be shut off to groups of people who feel disenfranchised, the cultural space is a place they can access easily and get into really quickly. Art is a very interesting area in which people can voice their dissent or their oppression, but it goes beyond that. Take a young person, for example, who has been through a very traumatic childhood – art can have a very transformational effect on how they look at and deal with that trauma. Through art you can be both artist and narrator, you take ownership of your experience, you take control of your situation and you can tell your story in the way that you want it to be told.

Gabrielle Tierney is Head of Community Initiatives at the Octavia Foundation. She is responsible for the charity's projects and activities including the employment, befriending and youth programmes.

GRAYSON PERRY

So, what does nobility mean to you?

It sounds old fashioned. Something that belongs to a different age of hierarchies and aristocracy, not something we talk about now. Sometimes you might meet a really posh person who is really nice and it's in their DNA to put other people first. There's something ethically pure about their integrity. But perhaps it's because they're so posh and rich that they never have to worry about their own circumstances. When you're struggling you become more selfish; you're going to fight for your place in the food bank queue if you're desperate. In some ways, nobility is a bit of a luxury. The idea of helping people is nice but I think it's something we do best when we've got the basics sorted.

So nobility is something that you can strive for only when your basic needs are met?

Yes. To ask any more of people is asking a bit much in my

opinion. Of course, there are extreme situations throughout history where people have been self-sacrificing, but the big issue in our society is that we've got enough – it's just not shared out right. This has an ignobling effect and we end up with a large section of society that feels it's ok to have two cars, three holidays, five computers and 48 pairs of high heels.

What do you think is the concept of nobility in a consumerist society?

Doing things we really don't want to do. Spending time with a boring relative, for example, where we put in the hours but swear we'll never do it again…until the next time! Essentially, humans want empirical evidence of things and consumerism gives us that – it's got a price, a brand, a measurement. That makes us happy. But are any of us any happier with that bigger house, with the better car and the nice shoes?

Do you think people can be encouraged to look beyond the materialistic?

As an artist I aspire to encourage people to see the world through different eyes. When I look at the world I notice things and then I make an artwork about that in the hope of raising public awareness of the things I've noticed and the processes I went through to get there. I enjoy the revelation and I want to pass it on. If we are moved by our deepest thoughts and feelings, we should try to pass that on to others.

What else can we do to be more noble as individuals, as a society?

I'm a bit suspicious about the dramatic nature of the nobility concept – as though I should go out there, completely change my life and set off to fight Ebola or something. Instead, society can benefit from lots of incremental changes and everyone doing their bit, however small. Paying tax is one of the noblest things we can do. Nobility should be mundane, an everyday occurrence; not this glamorous, celebrity-driven, shining knight stuff. It should be achievable.

Grayson Perry is an artist. Winner of the 2003 Turner Prize, he works with ceramics, bronze, printmaking and tapestry in unconventional ways, dealing with social issues such as class, sex and religion.

EDMUND LEWIS

Human beings aren't generally ones for living by themselves. We all enjoy the company of others. It's important to have a good community spirit; that was instilled in me by my headteacher at school. He always used to say that his favourite word was 'community' – that together in the school we could achieve great things. You need everybody to work together to have a happy home. Mixed communities are important too. I just think it's nice that there are people in our building who've lived in this particular bit of Westminster since they've been born. It would be highly unfair for people who've spent their whole lives in one area to be priced out. A diverse community brings a lot of history. Everyone has a right to live near their work and the facilities they require. Life's more fun with a mixed bunch.

Edmund Lewis has lived in London on and off for the past 31 years. He enjoys organising community parties at Peel House, the Octavia property in Pimlico where he is a shared ownership resident.

YASMIN ALIBHAI-BROWN

I am an exile. I have been an exile for most of my life. I was born, raised and educated in Uganda. I went to Makerere University for my first degree – a wonderful, stimulating institution. Then in 1972, Asians who had been there since the 19th century were thrown out by Idi Amin, the military dictator, helped into power by the UK, the US and Israel. This was during the Cold War when the Soviet Union and the West were waging their secret wars in Africa and elsewhere. So I found myself in Britain, a new and hostile land, but one that had a tremendous history and possibilities I would never have had in Uganda. Of course, my old homeland is always in my heart – the lush vegetation, red soil, lovely people – but I am part of my new homeland too.

When I was a child, I wanted to be an actress or writer. Somehow, through the years, I kept these dreams alive and though I never did get to act, I did find the courage to approach a newspaper at the age of 37 and persuade the editor that I could write. I was untrained, but burning with ideas and the urge to communicate. So here I am now, a proper journalist, with a column in *The Independent*, an author and broadcaster. Like all migrants, I worked hard and never let adversity stop me. I was lucky too.

One of the most precious consequences of having this public voice is hearing from other migrants and their truly noble lives. Rafa, for example, is an asylum seeker who was a midwife in her country – somewhere in the Middle East – and who quietly helps other asylum-seeking women deliver their babies, sometimes in the garage of a wonderful Englishwoman who tries to do her best for desperate people forced to flee. I have been called out twice to be present during births and that moment when a new life appears brings such joy. But I have witnessed not just the births but also the stoicism of the mothers as they go through labour without once screaming in pain. They do not want the neighbours disturbed or worried about what is going on.

Then there is Mo who, although he now has residence rights in the UK, had to leave his young family behind. He is taking GCSE exams after receiving home tutoring from a retired school teacher. In return for tuition, he takes care of the old man, whose own family does not visit him that often. Mo is 35, the old teacher is 78. Both have given each other something precious.

And, finally, Mary, a devout Christian from Uganda. She got in touch last year asking me to help her fill in forms. We became friends. She suffered terribly before she could get out of Uganda. I did not. Mary forgives her rapists and prays for their souls. I can't forgive Idi Amin for what he did but I am learning the art of forgiveness from her.

The noble lives of migrants are not seen, not known. I wish they were.

Yasmin Alibhai-Brown is a Uganda-born author. She is a leading commentator on race, multiculturalism and human rights. She writes regularly for *The Independent* and *The Guardian*.

CLAIRE LEVAVASSEUR

moved to the UK from Vincennes five years ago because of my husband's job. I was really keen to learn English, understand what people say – I like to be able to take part. And I believed that if my children were going to be raised here, it's important that we all learned the language.

What I wanted was to be able to have a regular chat in English with somebody English. So, instead of paying for language tuition, I thought it would be a good idea to chat with someone who wanted to spend some time talking to me. That's how I got involved in befriending. Kathleen and I meet every Thursday morning at around 10.30am. When we meet, we go grocery shopping. She puts her coat on and then we go to Waitrose. We get a taxi back and then sit down for coffee and biscuits. We used to have a Victoria sponge with fresh cream, but they don't do it anymore and she doesn't like the one with buttercream. I leave her about one o'clock.

Kathleen doesn't go out at all during the rest of the week. She has a taxi card to go places but she's afraid of other people a little bit. Once, she fell over in the street and so now she's not so confident. And she's nearly 90. She can do her own cooking and she does her washing – sheets, underwear, everything – in the sink because she doesn't have a washing machine.

I've got a good life compared to Kathleen's. I live in a big house near to a park. I'm lucky. It's nice to give something when you have so much yourself.

Befriending Kathleen has taught me that getting older isn't easy when you are alone. My grandfathers ended their lives with their family around them. Kathleen doesn't have people around. The time we spend together is important for her and fulfilling for me. I feel good going back home after I've seen her. We share that good feeling. She's funny and she's a really nice person. She tells me about London during the War. We had a FaceTime session with my sister the other day and Kathleen couldn't stop laughing because she'd never seen an iPhone. I showed her videos of my children skiing. She couldn't believe it and kept asking: 'Are they really skiing? Is that real?'

Often Kathleen struggles to get out of the taxi because she has short legs. The other day, the taxi driver tried to carry her and we laughed so much. We share lots of good moments. It's never sad or depressing, either for me or her.

Claire Levavasseur has been volunteering with the Octavia Foundation as a befriender for four years. She used to work as an architect in France before moving to London and is now a housewife.

FARIBA SHIRAZI

came to the UK in 2006 with my daughter following persecution in my home country of Iran. I had worked as a journalist there for 13 years but it was impossible for me to live there any more. I was arrested and tortured by the security services because I defended freedom, human rights and women's rights. It was the worst experience of my life.

So, I had to leave my country very quickly and it didn't take long for me to be granted asylum seeker status. But it was very difficult in the beginning. My English was not very good and I didn't know anything about London. My daughter was upset because she had no family and no friends around her. She lost everything when we left Iran and coping with the new life was very hard for her. We were fortunate enough to get a flat with Octavia Housing and we were supported not just by having a home but by the staff too. When I told them my story they said: 'Don't worry, we will help you. Don't feel that you are alone.' The next challenge was finding a school for my daughter. Unfortunately, she was bullied and because she didn't speak English, she struggled. Things have improved since then. The Octavia Foundation also gave me support to find a job with BBC Persia. I'm now an assistant editor and TV news presenter. Without their support I think it would have been impossible for me to get a job.

When I think back to the early days, everything was difficult. I was in an unfamiliar country, an unfamiliar home, I didn't know my neighbours. But when people found out that I had to come here from Iran, lots of people accepted it and said 'welcome' – they were all so helpful, supportive and gave me respect. I didn't face anyone who was angry or said 'Why did you come here?'

In the morning when I get the tube to work I see loads of different people. Not just British people – lots of skin colours, hairstyles, styles of dress, different cultures, different religions. The lot.

I think that, in London, the culture for immigrants is to accept other people patiently and respectfully, and then you will be accepted patiently and respectfully in return. Then we can all live together with peace and calm. In other countries there can be conflict because people have not accepted each other. I don't find this in London.

For example, when I'm on the escalator in an underground station, I walk on the left while people stand on the right. That is the culture. People accept it.

Fariba Shirazi has lived in an Octavia property with her daughter Kiana since 2006. She is an assistant editor and TV news presenter.

MARGARET BAILEY

My family are Irish and emigrated to Australia. I moved to the UK in 1979. I wouldn't have been able to live in London if I hadn't had access to social housing. That was especially the case when I split up from my husband and I was bringing up my child on my own. Whatever problems I had, a large percentage of them were resolved by having an affordable and secure place to live. We went from the awful situation of having nowhere to live to having a two-bedroomed place with a garden. Not having to worry about where I was going to live and how I could afford it gave me the chance to do, among other things, a Master's degree and continue my education. Social housing transformed our lives.

I find it hard to recognise the portrait painted of people who live in social housing – an underclass of people who do not accept responsibility for their lives and supporting their families. A lot of the families I know who live in social housing are working parents – and all seem to me to accept the responsibility of family and community.

When I moved into the area it was predominantly West Indian, Irish, Asian. My son benefitted from growing up in Kensal Rise – rich cultural experiences of diversity and difference. He has mixed in a very diverse community and I think that is an extremely positive thing.

I have been involved in the campaign to Save Kensal Rise Library. After five years of campaigning with the support of the community, we have managed to secure a space in the library building – rent-free in perpetuity.

The library has always been the centre of this community and its closure would have been a terrible loss for residents, many of whom live in social housing. The level of engagement from the community is still high today, even though the area has changed quite a bit and despite it being so expensive to rent or buy properties round here. The campaign has been a mixture of old and young, people with different political persuasions, high-income earners and no-income earners. I hope my involvement in the campaign has allowed me and others to challenge the misconceptions that the public have of social housing tenants.

One of the hardest things to achieve is confidence and being able to express your voice. That can be an issue for people who aren't university educated or who aren't used to having their opinions heard. My own background is working class. I'm in a very low paid job – it's low paid because it is in the community sector. But you don't work in that sector because you want a high income. You do it because of a commitment to an ideal and a desire to work with the people you live amongst. It's immensely rewarding.

The nursery that I work in was set up by local women who got together because they didn't think there was childcare around that met the needs of their children. They were committed to working towards an ideal and achieving it. We're still here after 30 years with a waiting list that's endless! It's an example of women taking control of their environment, just as Octavia Hill did 150 years ago.

Octavia Hill made a lot of sacrifices and I am inspired by women like her. Choosing a path that benefits the whole community, as Octavia did, is a noble choice. Thanks to her work, I have a secure place to live and this has given me the courage to do inspirational things myself. I'd like to thank her for the chances she's given me.

I think it's particularly inspiring that, 150 years on, there are still opportunities to follow her lead to tackle similar social challenges, give commitment to an idea or cause or encourage groups of people to do something for the community. I like that sense of continuity, seeing people unified by a common ideal. It's an important link to the past and an important message for the future.

Margaret Bailey has lived in Kensal Rise for over thirty years. She is the manager of a community nursery in Kensal Green. She is also Chair of the Save Kensal Rise Library campaign.

BEATRIX CAMPBELL

Octavia Hill is a wondrous exemplar of that great English phenomenon: a contradiction. She pioneered physical presence in social work and social housing – highlighting the importance of the personal visit and of personal, proximate management of dwellings. But her innovations, whilst progressive, exposed the narrow coordinates of her theory and practice: presence was framed by sympathy rather than empathy, by discipline rather than democracy. She championed the virtue of autonomy, but she stripped social power from her concept of self-reliance. Her notion of society as one big family could be enlisted in the Thatcherite maxim – there is no such thing as society, only individuals and families – though that would traduce the best of her intentions. She recognised 'home' as more than a roof, she regarded dwellings as social spaces where the material provides both shelter and sanitation and a life; she also recognised social living as a system that needs to be made and maintained – in short, to be managed.

However, Octavia Hill did not recognise that families, like communities and nations, are characterised by need, care and *power*. Hill witnessed the travails of women in general, and mothers in particular, but did not translate sympathy into social radicalism and, in particular, into support for universal suffrage. Her legacy lives on, not least in the welfare state that she so fiercely resisted. Her heroic endeavours have nobility and yet expose their own limits – the very limits that provoke the democratic spirit, social solidarity and the modern welfare state.

Beatrix Campbell is a writer, broadcaster and activist. She has written for *The Guardian* and *New Statesman*, among others, and is the author of nine books.

THE RT HON.
THE BARONESS GREY-THOMPSON

As President of the National Council for Voluntary Organisations I believe, like Octavia Hill, that individuals can bring about positive social change. Every day, thousands of people across Britain give their time, energy and expertise to support voluntary organisations in an attempt to make a real difference to the lives of others – and in doing so they are helping to build stronger, healthier and more cohesive communities.

Octavia's volunteers were concentrated in her social housing model but volunteering permeates all aspects of our lives. Lots of sports initiatives and organisations, for example, rely on volunteers to help out and, quite frankly, I wouldn't have had a sporting career if it hadn't been for the dedication of the volunteers who agreed to coach me, as a teenager, growing up in South Wales. The coaches and organisers at local sports clubs are incredibly important – particularly in recognising talent and encouraging young people to be healthy and fit. The army of Games Makers at the London 2012 Olympic and Paralympic Games were the key to the success of the event.

Although opinion may be divided on Octavia Hill's message, her use of volunteers to educate, inform and guide her social housing tenants is a lesson that modern society has grasped, and is using to great effect.

The Rt Hon. the Baroness Grey-Thompson is Britain's most successful Paralympic athlete. She has won 11 gold medals in wheelchair racing in five consecutive Games. Since retiring from competitive sport, Tanni has taken an active role in the House of Lords, particularly on disability rights.

PHILOMENA DOMINIQUE

Before I came to Octavia, I used to drive minibuses transporting adults and children with special needs. My physical disability had not yet started causing limitations to my everyday life, so in 2007, I became a Professional Service Vehicle driver. I learnt all about driving legislation and rules and really enjoyed it, but by the middle of 2010 I was finding it physically challenging. My life was all about driving and I only stopped because, physically, I couldn't do it anymore. I remember thinking: 'What am I going to do now? I am only 50 years old – where do I go, what do I do?'

I have been volunteering since September 2010. At first there were barriers to overcome but over the past four or five years I've grown in confidence and I've been empowered. My focus now is my involvement in what's going on in the community and to show people that just because you have a disability doesn't mean that your life ends. There are things you can do, things you can learn.

Volunteering has enabled me to learn new things and I've grown as a person due to the fact that I've gone on to get a new qualification. If your mind is active, everyday life improves and your overall outlook on life improves. I'm not saying that I don't have my bad days but it's important to me to be proactive in accepting my limitations and going on to do other things despite my limitations, if that makes sense. If you cut yourself off from your community, the way I look at it is that you are only harming yourself.

Volunteering gives you a real sense of achievement. Sometimes I think: 'My goodness, look what I've achieved!' Instead of dwelling on my own situation, volunteering allows me to empower somebody else and make them more aware of what's available to them. I'm giving encouragement, support and time to somebody else. I don't want to sound patronising but it gives me a good feeling to go home knowing that I helped somebody – I never thought I'd have that kind of effect on other people. It's rewarding to know that I've enabled them to see that there is help out there and that life is never as bad as they think it is.

Philomena Dominique has been a long-term volunteer with the Octavia Foundation, assisting their Employment and Training Team.

THE RT HON.
THE LORD CARNWATH

Octavia Hill was passionately committed to the protection of the environment. She believed that all urban workers, however poor, should have access to open spaces: 'Places to sit in, places to play in, places to stroll in, and places to spend a day in.' As someone who has worked all his professional life on issues of planning and environmental law, I feel a special attraction to this part of her legacy. I see her as the forerunner of so many noble campaigners, whom I have come to know and admire in both my professional and personal life, and who have battled – like her – to protect and improve our urban and rural environment.

She was instrumental in helping to save Hampstead Heath and Parliament Hill Fields from development. She was, it is said, the first to use the term 'green belt' for the protected rural areas surrounding London. She was also active outside London; in 1883, for example, she campaigned to stop the construction of railways in sight of Buttermere in the Lake District.

One of her greatest contributions was in founding the National Trust in 1895. It has since become one of the UK's largest landowners – and its largest membership organisation – dedicated to preserving places of natural beauty or historic interest for the public in perpetuity. Jumping forward more than a century, the pressures for development to meet the needs of a growing population and a growing economy have become even more intense and demanding. We are fortunate that the immediate post-war government established, in the Town and Country Planning Acts, a powerful and effective framework for what we now call 'sustainable development'. But it was the inspired efforts of campaigners who used that framework to force politicians, administrators and developers to live up to these aspirations. There have been failures, yes, but so many successes.

To take but a few examples, it is difficult now to believe that less than 50 years ago (about the time I started working in the law), the London Plan proposed the demolition of most of Covent Garden to make way for modern development and a major relief road for the Strand. A few determined individuals gained the ear of a sympathetic Secretary of State, who had the key buildings listed overnight. In more recent times, we have seen the Thames opened up for public use and enjoyment in an imaginative combination of public and private efforts. At Bankside, we have seen a power station converted into one of the world's most successful art galleries, open to all, which has acted as a catalyst for the regeneration of a whole area. The Millennium Bridge provides direct access to St Paul's Cathedral on the opposite bank, beyond which Paternoster Square has been transformed by an elegant development incorporating the reinstated 17th-century Temple Bar.

Through the efforts of Octavia Hill and those who have followed her, London remains a wonderful place in which to work, live and enjoy life. *Si monumentum requiris, circumspice!**

Lord Carnwath is a Justice at the UK Supreme Court.
Between 2007 and 2012 he was Senior President of Tribunals.
His background is in environmental law.

* 'If you seek his monument, look around you.'

SIR SIMON JENKINS

One of Hill's great passions was the outdoors. She saw open country as a delight, a therapy and, indeed, a right for those 'imprisoned' in Victorian cities. 'We all want beauty for the refreshment of our souls,' she wrote in the 1880s. 'Sometimes we think of it as a luxury, but when God made the world, he made it very beautiful and meant that we should live amongst its beauties, and that they should speak peace to us in our daily lives.'

Many had long complained against the pace of industrialisation, not least John Ruskin to whom Hill was initially a loyal acolyte. Hill had risen through the Commons Preservation Society and, in 1876, became the treasurer of the Kyrle Society, founded by her eldest sister, Miranda, 'for the diffusion of beauty'. It aimed to bring art, books, music and, above all, open spaces into the lives of the urban poor.

Hill soon became an articulate and ruthless campaigner against the march of development across the suburban landscape, initially round London. While she failed to save the fields of Swiss Cottage from the building of Fitzjohns Avenue, her ferocity and skill at marshalling powerful allies fuelled the subsequent campaign for Hampstead Heath.

In 1894, Hill joined the Cumbrian clergyman, Hardwick Rawnsley, and a quiet solicitor named Robert Hunter to found the National Trust, aimed at 'preserving places of historic interest or natural beauty'. This combination of goals was crucial to British conservation, eliding past and present, history and aesthetics in a noble concept of rounded social value.

Hill's zeal would eventually yield Britain's national parks, green belts, rural planning and 'right to roam'. They gave our densely-populated island a clear legal distinction between town and country, protecting the latter in Britain's greatest contribution to planning practice. Hill taught that this protection would not emerge from a free market in land or from the give and take of democracy. It had to be championed by people who cared.

Philanthropic, non-conformist, innovative and persistent, Octavia Hill made an enormous impact on Victorian society in many ways; yet it is her commitment to the preservation and enjoyment of the great outdoors that marked her out as being well ahead of her time. Her endeavours back then paved the way for us all to enjoy Britain's natural heritage today and for our children to enjoy in the future. Octavia's legacy is not just awareness of the value of nature and of the role beauty should play in our lives. It is that such awareness means nothing if not fought for. And with our ever-increasing population, her legacy has never been more needed than today.

Sir Simon Jenkins is a journalist and author who writes for *The Guardian*. He was Chairman of the National Trust from 2008–2014.

SANDI TOKSVIG

I once came across a Victorian gardening book which, under the heading 'Wild Flowers', contained the wonderful phrase: 'No matter how small your garden, do try and devote a couple of acres to wild flowers.' What a heavenly thought. How splendid to have a couple of spare acres hanging about waiting for a purpose. I think of such riches whenever I see a small window box hanging from a ledge on a giant block of flats or a single flowerpot standing on an urban doorstep. There is something so life affirming, so very noble about a bit of green, a blossom or a hint of wild planting in a city scape. I am grateful to those who bother and share their efforts with others. In fact, my gratitude is so great that some years ago it nearly got me arrested.

My former mother-in-law is called Joy. Although the relationship which brought me into her life has transformed itself into friendship, Joy and I continue, somehow, to be family to each other. Joy is – or perhaps I need to say was, for the years keep her more sedentary now – a passionate gardener. For a period of time she owned a flat which overlooked a public common with a tiny duck pond.

'They don't keep it properly,' she would say each time I visited. 'They should plant flowers round the edge and keep it tidier.' Joy phoned the council but could find no one to agree. So, before I had ever heard of it anywhere else, Joy, ever the feisty soul, took up guerilla gardening. Late at night she would sneak across to the pond and plant daffodil bulbs round the edge. Under the light of the moon she would trim back bushes and introduce bull rushes. Local people began to comment on how nice the pond was looking and how the rest of the common might benefit. They praised the council for doing the job so discreetly and Joy smiled but kept quiet.

One night she asked me to bring over my ancient lawnmower which operated only by human power. 'You don't have a lawn,' I said, rather reasonably. 'Come anyway,' she replied.

And so I found myself, around midnight, trimming the grass path that led to the pond. It was surprisingly pleasing to garden late at night when others had long gone to bed. It was pleasing until a local police car cruised past. 'Coppers!' shouted Joy and we hid behind a tree leaving the lawnmower looking like a piece of installation art on the path. They drove on but a few days later Joy got a letter from the council accusing her of trespass. It broke her heart and soon after she moved away. I drive past that place occasionally and I always think of her and her noble – but secret – task of making things more beautiful for everyone.

Long live guerilla gardeners.

Sandi Toksvig is a TV and radio presenter and a writer. She regularly appears on TV shows such as *QI* and presents Radio 4's *The News Quiz*.

PETER WOOD

When you think about it, it's clear what a wonderful woman Octavia must have been – always thinking about other people, always putting them first. She must have been very courageous to do the work she did, as a woman, all those years ago. She wanted to make sure people saw a bit of green around, too, didn't she? A garden is very rewarding because you can see things growing and see what you've achieved. You get real personal pleasure with a garden. Outside space, to me, is like a shop window. If you see an attractive shop window, it encourages you to go in. Having a bit of green around makes a difference to how you feel. You get pleasure going outside and seeing shrubs and flowers growing but if you live in a block where it's just block after block – like a concrete jungle – you don't get that sense of appreciation.

I sometimes think that people enjoyed a more happy home life in the past than they do now. Nowadays, homes are full of gadgets and what have you. Everyone these days is connected to – what are they called? –

Twitter and all that sort of thing. Has that made life happier? I don't think so. Technology is a wonderful invention, but it stops us talking to each other. Like, for instance, if you want to complain to the gas people or the electricity people, you can't speak to someone any more. It's all recorded messages and that proves quite difficult for a lot of elderly people. They don't understand it and can get confused; it's much better to be able to deal with people. We save money by having recorded messages but then we talk about needing to get more people into work. It's all the wrong way round.

Peter Wood is a resident of an Octavia property in Ladbroke Grove, where he also works as a gardener. Originally from Blackpool, he has lived in London for more than 40 years. He is a retired cabin service officer.

EILEEN ROSS

have lived here seven years. I love it, and I love the garden. The garden is my pride and joy. It's a very busy part of the city, just between London Bridge and Waterloo, and we get a lot of people walking up and down Sudrey Street. A lot of them are tourists and they shout in, 'We love your garden!' and I reply, 'Thank you!'

Everyone says to me: 'You're always out in the garden.' I've met lots of friends through being out in the garden. It's lovely how people will stop and talk. I'm on my own and doing the garden is therapeutic for me. Every summer I bring cushions out and I sit and look back at my place and I say to myself: 'Do you know something? I feel as though I'm on holiday, this is a holiday cottage!' I really do feel as though I'm on holiday because there is no sign of London here.

But I've got London on the brain. I love London! When you're in London you're never really on your own – there's always someone to talk to. I've met people at the bus stop and because I see them there on a regular basis, we've become friends. I talk to everyone, even the road sweepers. I always stop and say good morning to them.

I think Octavia Hill was a fantastic girl. Starting out at her young age with such plans in mind was incredible. She must have been a great lady to achieve what she did, that's all I can say. I've always said that, always.

Eileen Ross is an Octavia resident living in Gable Cottages, a late 19th-century residence in Southwark. She is a retired nurse from County Clare in Ireland. In 2008, her efforts in the cottage gardens were rewarded with a prize from Southwark in Bloom for best community garden.

SIR CRISPIN TICKELL

It has been said that ours is the first generation that can end poverty and the last one that can avoid the worst impacts of climate change. Octavia Hill addressed poverty and the environment 150 years ago. Why are we still dealing with these issues?

We must consider the factors which make for poverty – the exhaustion of resources, human proliferation and the many other things that humans are doing to the surface of the earth. If we can correct these things, we can certainly alleviate poverty. But human proliferation means that we're not going to get rid of poverty very quickly, if ever. At the moment, population is growing at a rate which means poverty will be increased in many parts of the world. Regarding climate change, some things we can address, some we can't. Reducing carbon emissions could make a big difference but some things are past the point of no return – particularly oceans. The rise of temperature and sea levels is something we can never change.

Do you think there is any need for a change of attitudes and ambition if we are going to achieve a more sustainable world?

I think that one of the most damaging things is the way that politicians talk about the need for economic growth in terms of constantly producing more things. The target should be to produce a balance of society in which there is no great deprivation or poverty at the bottom of the scale, but a reasonable flexibility at the top. When I was running the government panel on sustainability I posed the question: 'Are we treating the earth as if we intended to stay?' We are not, but I think that people are becoming increasingly aware of it. You have got to be aware of the interests of the community and the other people with whom you share the planet.

Do you think there is any place for the aspiration of a noble life in the 21st-century?

Yes I do. I think that living a full and balanced life with due care for others is one of the most important things. We need to have fulfilment of basic ambitions, enough to eat and drink, however, we also need to be able to do things on an intellectual basis. There has been a lot of doubt expressed about whether human civilisation could survive in the longer term. I am optimistic about the intellectual capacity of humans to improve things but I am pessimistic about our will to do so.

Have we lacked progress as a society?

We have made more progress in pursuing material wealth than we have in pursuing a balanced society because it is easier. That's because people like to have concrete, practical objectives, whereas general community welfare is very difficult to define. For many years, I was President of Tree Aid which was concerned with planting trees and reducing deforestation. The problem was this: if somebody offers you a lot of money for wood, you will cut the tree down. But the long-term result is that with no forests, there is no water. This is an example of commercial advantage being one thing and the longer-term welfare of society being quite another.

***

Sir Crispin Tickell is a former British diplomat and a leading international authority on climate change and environmental issues, on which he advised successive British Prime Ministers.

ANN HAWTHORN

have got a lot of memories from World War II. I remember being in Chippenham in Wiltshire with my mum and seeing lots of Italian prisoners of war working on the land. One of them looked at me and said to my mum: 'I got a bambino back in Italy.' Another time we were walking up a country lane and we saw some American airmen. One of them took a lollipop out of his pocket, pulled the paper off and handed it to me. It was like a sugary bowl on a stick. Seeing these men made my mum a bit upset. She said: 'I'm sure, like us, they'd much rather be at home with their wives and children.' I can also remember what it was like inside the Anderson shelter. The space was very restricted. It was narrow and just a place to sit really. The old lady who owned the house, she was Scottish and she liked a drop of whisky, and every time it sounded as though a bomb had gone off, she'd say to my mum: 'I think it's been a direct hit. You go outside and check Mrs Hawthorn, you're more nimble than I am. See if me house has gone.' It's awful to think that we had six years of it. 'Oh, don't worry,' they said, when the war started. 'It'll be over in three weeks time, we'll soon lick the Germans.' But instead it went on for six years. I don't know how we came through everything when I think about it – all the rationing and everything.

I'm one of these people who likes their own company. I always have been. When I was at school, one of the teachers wrote on my report that I was of a 'fairly retiring disposition'. I'll never forget that. I suffered a mild stroke not so long ago and I hardly went out last summer. So I said to my brother: 'I don't want to be stuck indoors all the time, I'd like to go out and about.' I asked him if he could get me some maps a week or two ago. He's going to take some photocopies from the A–Z so I can visit the three parks that were close to my last address – Avondale Park, Kensington Memorial Park and Holland Park. Now I've got the strength back in my legs and I've got this walker, I can get out and do a bit of shopping. I've also got a Freedom Pass and a taxi card, so I can go to Baker Street where I used to live and go to a restaurant now and again. Of all the properties I've lived in, this one is the best. It's nicely decorated and there's help and support if I need it. I don't often need it but it's there, you know?

Ann Hawthorn is a resident at Leonora House, one of Octavia's extra care schemes in Maida Vale. She has lived in London all her life.

"NOBILITY IS WHEN AN INDIVIDUAL BECOMES SOMETHING BIGGER, SOMETHING MORE WORTHWHILE. SOMETHING THAT WILL BENEFIT THE WHOLE OF SOCIETY."

Fiona Reynolds

DEBORAH MEADEN

Octavia Hill spoke of her ambition to make 'lives noble, homes happy and family life good'. What does the word noble mean to you?

I actually use the word noble quite often. To me, something is noble if it is notable, exceptional and selfless. The motivation to be noble might, simply, be to 'do the right thing' but on a deeper level it could be someone's personal sacrifice. Being noble is to do something worthy of merit, with honour. But acting nobly doesn't have to be big. It can start as a small thing and gain traction.

Does the concept of being noble crop up in business ?

Yes it does – and not just when talking about other entrepreneurs. To me, being noble depends on the action, not the person. If I am working with someone who has done something notable, exceptional or selfless I will not hesitate to tell them that they have done the right thing or have acted for the right reasons. I like the word noble. What's interesting about it is that you can describe its meaning using many other words, but none are quite sufficient to encapsulate its full sentiment.

Do you consider entrepreneurship to be noble at all?

I do, but not per se. I certainly wouldn't describe every entrepreneur as a noble person but when someone decides to do something to further their own life and their family's lives, and in the process of doing so creates jobs, contributes to industry and boosts the economy, then I would describe that as noble. Entrepreneurs are not afraid to create their own culture, focus on their core values and embrace opportunities to create change. That too, in my opinion, is noble.

Many successful businesses these days are values-driven. How important is that?

Extremely. I think the world is becoming a better place because we increasingly demand honesty. The days where an organisation can say one thing and do the opposite are gone. People don't like it. This culture shift is fantastic because it makes people think about how they behave, beyond generating profits. But being noble in business is not just about asking yourself 'Is this the right thing to do?' – it's about acting on the response.

Octavia Hill was an entrepreneur. What do you think her achievements mean in a modern context?

Octavia was ahead of her time. She set her own goals and her own rules to make life better for those less well off. And she had confidence, the single biggest requirement in business. Taking action for reasons other than personal gain is undeniably noble and Octavia's work personifies that.

If you were to meet Octavia today, what would you say to her?

I wouldn't say anything. I would sit and listen to her because she was a woman with vision, with clarity and with all the right motivations. She did that very special thing that most of us aspire to; she left this world a better place because she was in it. When she came across obstacles she didn't stop. She went over them, around them – whatever was necessary to achieve her aims.

Deborah Meaden is a businesswoman who has become a household name through her role in BBC2's *Dragon's Den*. She started her first business aged 19. She is now a full-time investor with a portfolio ranging from fashion to waste management.

DAME FIONA REYNOLDS

'To make individual life noble, homes happy and family life good.' These words are typical Octavia Hill. She had a striking capacity for seeing life in the round: she knew that people needed the basic requirements of life, but also that they needed to be surrounded by beauty and good things, like nature and open spaces. Furthermore, Octavia was always grounded in morality – life would not be fulfilling if it were not founded on goodness.

We express ourselves differently today, but we need the same things. We all know that the human spirit needs more than that which money can buy, even if our economic system finds this difficult to account for. And we also know that a happy childhood is important to our future life prospects.

It's that word 'noble' we struggle with, because it has fallen out of everyday use. But I still think we can see what she meant. Throughout my career, mostly in the voluntary sector and largely in the National Trust, I have felt inspired by Octavia Hill's legacy and moral leadership –

by her nobility. Moreover, I think she ennobled all of us in the movement by association; we often asked ourselves (sometimes rhetorically), 'What would Octavia have done?' and simply asking that question made us think more nobly, generously and deeply about the moral basis for our actions and decisions.

Now that I've left the National Trust and am involved in education, I feel I carry Octavia's spirit, if anything, even more deeply in my heart. She cared passionately about education and ran a school with her sisters early in her life; one of her early campaigns was getting the Cambridge Local Examinations Board to accept entries from girls. Today, I'm living in an ancient and beautiful Cambridge college, surrounded by stellar academics and enthusiastic students. It's a joy to be in a place where learning is valued for its own sake, and where there is no cynicism about striving for the highest standards of achievement. But that is not enough: what enriches life here beyond measure is the sense of community, commitment to each other and a generosity of spirit that subsumes the whole place. I watch students from every background thrive, not only through their intellectual development but through their growing sense of responsibility for themselves and each other, and the development of values that will shape their whole lives. Nobility stems from doing the right things for the right reasons.

Education remains, in fact, the great liberator. It equips us in so many tangible ways for life, but it also frees our spirit to be the people we want to be. It is our duty as a society to ensure that everyone has access to education, and the chance to flourish. But it will reap more rewards than simply personal ones. Nobility, as Octavia recognised, is that point where an individual becomes something bigger, something more worthwhile – something that will benefit the whole of society.

Dame Fiona Reynolds was Director-General of the National Trust from 2001–2012. She is now Master of Emmanuel College, Cambridge.

MAX ROBSON

After I finished school I was out of education, out of work. I wanted to pursue filmmaking and one day a flyer on the floor caught my eye. It was promoting *Grove Roots*, a documentary about the history of Ladbroke Grove made by volunteer young, local filmmakers through the Octavia Foundation. I've always lived in and around that area so I decided to go to one of the screenings at the youth group. I was impressed and knew immediately that I wanted to work with them – I let them know that if they had any other projects, I'd love to get involved.

Eventually, they called me in for a meeting. I talked about my experience and said that I would love to volunteer with them on a film they were producing called *Hidden Herstories*. I went on every shoot. It was a full-time commitment but it kick-started the idea that it could be a reality that I could make films, produce interesting work.

People have asked me why I volunteered but the volunteers involved get so much from working on these projects. It was one of the most valuable times of my life and I met so many inspiring people.

During the making of *Hidden Herstories*, I learned a lot about Octavia Hill. It opened my eyes to what's important. Her ethos of helping people to help themselves was a ground-breaking attitude for the time and the fact that she empowered people to take responsibility for themselves rather than simply give them money was brilliant. She taught me that 'you give people an inch and you get back a mile'. I've visited the areas that she built up and the properties seem like such lovely places to live – better than these massive high-rises. Stacking people up on top of each other, surrounded by concrete, is not a pleasant way to organise people.

Octavia talked of noble lives. And the thing is, I don't think face-to-face she was especially pleasant. She wasn't interested in fluffy conversations, she wouldn't have wrapped you up in cotton wool and given you a cup of tea. What she was interested in was achieving action and progress in a firm but fair way – 'tough love' we call it these days. I feel very lucky to have been surrounded by noble people growing up. They showed me an alternative way at a difficult time in my life. Being a teenager is always complicated – you don't know what you want to do, how you want to grow, you're angry. Having positive role models lifted me up and kept me going. I feel honoured that I had a nice home life and lots of support. The people I've met and the things I've learned have inspired me to give something back to my community.

Max Robson is a young filmmaker who has lived in Kensal Rise for 23 years. After studying film, he worked as a lighting designer while producing short films and music promos before working with Octavia in 2014 on their media project *The Story of QPR*.

JOHN BIRD

The Victorian era produced some great people – far greater, in my opinion, than those produced today – including, for example, the indomitable traveller Isobel Bird (no relation); John Ruskin, the one-man army who sought to bestow a renaissance roundedness upon everyone, whatever their class; and the dogged and passionate Octavia Hill – social campaigner, housing reformer and nature champion.

I discovered Octavia whilst researching social responses to housing and homelessness. I rediscovered her when I looked into the creation of the National Trust and the late Victorian campaigns around the social justice issue of protecting nature so that all of us, irrespective of our social standing, could enjoy its inspiration.

When I started *The Big Issue* I did it using Octavia as a model. She understood that social justice was as much about the bricks and mortar around you as the education you received and the work that you carried out. She bought land and built houses and began to raise the issue of reform through practical applications of housing justice.

At that time, most housing stock available to the hardworking poor was substandard, unhealthy and expensive. So why did Octavia invest in housing for working people and build superior stock when she could have made a fortune stuffing the people into slums? She did so because she was ahead of her time; because she was both entrepreneurial and socially responsible.

It is hard to believe that, back in the 1880s, Marylebone had many slums. Octavia moved in and built superior housing for hardworking poor people; and she did it as a business. She made it wash its own face in the same way that, many decades later, I started *The Big Issue* and have made it self-sufficient ever since.

Over a decade ago I looked out of the window of my Marylebone flat and saw a blue plaque commemorating Octavia. At that time I lived in a block that backed onto Octavia's first experiments in the business of social housing. I felt incredibly privileged that I was so close to her social experiment, to her entrepreneurial social endeavour.

I am not a historian but I am a passionate believer in a world that people like Octavia Hill fought for: a world where all of us have the opportunity to share nature and society; where all of us – whether we use a hammer or a pen – can feel included.

I only wish she was around for us today, for housing and social inclusion is, once more, at a premium.

Octavia cannot and will not be forgotten, so long as there is someone whose life is narrowed by the housing in which they live. As long as there is injustice in housing, the spirit of Octavia will remind us that it could – and should – be done better and that we need not accept less for those who deserve more.

John Bird is the founder of *The Big Issue*, the world's most successful street magazine. Born into poverty and raised in social care, he was a prison inmate, artist and poet before becoming a political activist and author.

ALDO WILLIAMS

When I first moved into my housing association home it was such a nice feeling. The neighbours were really nice – a mix of general needs and shared ownership alongside privately-owned property.

I chose to live in London because of my job; I work in health care. I also chose London because I'm gay and I don't want to live in a homophobic part of the country. It's important to feel secure in your home and engaged in your neighbourhood. I can't go down Marylebone High Street without people stopping me and saying hello. My partner calls me 'Mr Popular'! But so many people are being pushed out of London. It should not be a privilege to live here – you should be able to live where you work, where you provide services. We need to do a lot more in our society to ensure that people can live near to where they work and that it's affordable. In my job I see excellent doctors travelling in to central London from Dagenham or Walthamstow and when they get to work they are tired. I see children travelling on the tube for over an hour to get to school. It just doesn't make sense to me.

I don't like the word noble. I think it's very dated, condescending. I think Octavia meant it in the sense that people didn't have *hope* in those days because they lived in squalor. She gave them hope that they – anyone – could have a different life. For her, it was about aspiration and doing the best for society in general. And it's the same today – breaking down barriers and giving people hope, aspirations and dreams. People can make their lives better but they've got to put some effort in.

We need to empower people to do more, for themselves, for the community. We need to give people the skills to respect themselves rather than set them up to fail. If people are to be happy they need the skills to deal with life and to be independent. Having a home is great but it won't make you happy. Independence, coping skills – learning how to cope with society and what life throws at you – these are the building blocks for happiness.

Aldo Williams is an Octavia resident who has lived in Westminster for 20 years. He has a Doctorate in Public Health and has worked for the NHS as a Health Visitor for the homeless and asylum seekers in Westminster.

DOROTHY DELAHUNT

To me, social housing should be available when people really need it, but when they don't they should be encouraged to move up the ladder. As a society we should want people to move up the ladder to some extent. I know it's not always possible but we need to enable people to get to the point where they are self-sufficient – that, to me, is the whole point of social housing. Octavia Hill was a woman well ahead of her time because she looked at life holistically and saw how home life, the great outdoors, mobility and autonomy each played a part in producing responsible citizens.

Being a responsible citizen and living a noble life is about dignity – living a dignified life but also being recognised as worthy of respect. Respect for being someone who has achieved their potential, who acts for others and who gives of themselves. The concept of living a dignified life is quite an old-fashioned ideal and these days so many people cheapen themselves through their behaviour and their lack of respect for themselves and others. If we have respect for ourselves we are entitled to demand it from other people because of our actions and how we commit to the world.

The problem with London nowadays is that it's crammed. London is heaving with people yet essential services are gradually being reduced. Police stations have been sold off, fire stations are closing, magistrates' courts have been demolished and hospitals are being razed to the ground. We're putting more and more people in but we are not serving them properly. It is irresponsible. London is going to become New York – a sterile, soulless, sanitised city of the rich.

Dorothy Delahunt is an Octavia resident who has lived in Westminster for 14 years. She is a business owner.

PROFESSOR DAME CAROL BLACK

For most people, work is a determinant of self-worth, identity and dignity, their capability to support a family and secure their esteem and their standing within the community, besides material progress and a means of social participation and fulfilment.

As National Director for Health and Work and subsequently, my chief preoccupations have been twofold – the impact of the health and wellbeing of working-age people upon their working lives and the impact of the workplace upon their health and wellbeing.

Numerous factors influence health and wellbeing and there-fore, employment outcomes. Some are deeply embedded in the fabric of society, amenable to change and amelioration but often only slowly.

My concern has been more immediate – to focus on the needs of people whose impaired health already affects their working lives. For many people, sustained worklessness –

from any cause – is itself followed by impaired physical or mental health and general wellbeing.

Integral to addressing these problems has been to view health and work as a collaborative enterprise. It is an enterprise in which governments, healthcare and social agencies, welfare agencies, employers and individuals each recognise their responsibilities in enabling productive and rewarding work for people with physical and mental health problems whilst safeguarding and promoting sustained good health in those who are well.

Employee engagement not only draws together the goals and aspirations of employees and employers, it is recognised as essential to achieving them. Engagement, or its absence, is evident in attitudes, behaviours, working relationships and organisational arrangements. It determines the ambience of the workplace, at every level, affecting the outward signs of human wellbeing and, no less, of service and performance. Cultural change is needed if we are to raise levels of health and wellbeing, and morale, of working-age people. I am confident that such change has begun.

Professor Dame Carol Black is the Department of Health's Expert Advisor on improving the welfare of working people. She is Principal of Newnham College, Cambridge and Chair of the Nuffield Trust.

THE RT HON.
THE LORD ADONIS

What does the word noble mean for you?

To me, being noble means creating good communities or enhancing existing communities through worthwhile projects. Take housing, for example: we are all aware that we need more of it, but what we really need is good housing that brings together mixed communities and doesn't create ghettos for either the rich or the poor. Housing projects that embrace these ideals are vital to strong community life and are noble, worthwhile causes.

Another example is social work. Through my work as chair of Frontline, I encounter many vulnerable families whose future happiness depends on support from effective social workers; therefore, making social work a career choice for more graduates is a priority for me. The ability of good social workers to turn failing families into successful families is, like community-driven housing projects, an essential part of creating happy homes and good family life – another noble cause.

One of Octavia Hill's objectives was to address poverty but 150 years on it still exists. Why do you think that is?

All societies have to confront social and economic problems. But even though we can improve conditions over time – and conditions for people are infinitely better than they were in Victorian Britain – family breakdown and relative poverty levels remain unacceptably high. There are many reasons for this – housing shortages, population pressures, economic downturns – and each generation has to confront the issues anew. We will never live in a perfect society where such challenges don't exist. We just have to do our best – as Octavia did.

What do you think Octavia would make of today's social welfare climate?

I think she would be pleasantly surprised. In her day, most working-class people lived in appalling conditions with no public support for health, education or welfare, and I think she would be pleased that some of these problems have been tackled, despite her opposition to the notion of a welfare state. She would certainly recognise modern social problems as being similar to those she sought to eradicate, in particular lack of opportunity for many people from less-privileged backgrounds.

What do you think the next generation of social reformers will look like?

I rather hope that the next generation will develop social reform into an established profession, like the legal profession, for example. This would give it a more solid framework within which social challenges can be tackled holistically; after all, many social problems are intrinsically linked – as they were in Octavia's day – yet are still separately addressed.

If we are to crack our social challenges, we must also regard dealing with social problems as important as making money and having a pleasant life. For many people from well-off backgrounds, addressing social problems just isn't on their horizon, whereas people who come from more disadvantaged backgrounds tend to have more empathy but may lack the means to take action. If we are to continue reforming society in the spirit of Octavia Hill, our aim must be to become one nation and work together – irrespective of background – to overcome the huge social inequalities that still exist in modern society.

Lord Adonis is a Labour peer who served as Minister for Schools and Transport Secretary under Tony Blair and Gordon Brown. He currently sits on the front bench in the House of Lords as the Shadow Infrastructure Minister.

"A NOBLE PERSON
NEVER FORGETS
WHERE THEY HAVE
COME FROM.
AND THEY NEVER
FORGET THE CAUSE."

Jasvinder Sanghera

JULIA UNWIN

Octavia Hill had high ambitions for people and places in poverty. The aspirations for nobility, happiness and good family life are as relevant today as they ever were and, indeed, an expression of her views could serve brilliantly as a mission statement for most charities, housing associations and public bodies in the UK today.

However, her powerful words only serve to remind me of how much we have lost. It is hard to imagine a life less noble than the one lived by so many people in poverty. Offered only extremely precarious work, insecure in their housing and vilified in the press, the lack of dignity experienced by people in poverty in 21st-century Britain would have appalled Octavia Hill. The nobility of work described by 19th-century social reformers is mocked by the insecurity facing the poorest people in our society today. The notion of a stable home – so central to our expectations of a decent and productive life – is challenged by short-term and expensive tenancies, and the bonds of family life are weakened by the demands of a voracious economy and our current approach to welfare reform.

And yet through the ages, Octavia Hill's words still pack a powerful punch. To aspire to live well, to have a stable home, to care for the people you love and be cared for in return are ambitions we all share, and it remains the purpose of both organisations and individuals to ensure that this is possible. In our much more diverse society, enabled by digital capability that Octavia Hill could never have imagined, we have the opportunity to build strong communities where people can flourish, and where individual dignity and power are supported. She provides a timely reminder for all of us about what really matters in life.

Julia Unwin is Chief Executive of the Joseph Rowntree Foundation, which investigates and addresses the causes of social problems and poverty, and the Joseph Rowntree Housing Trust.

THE RT HON.
THE LORD HOWARD

What does the phrase 'a noble life' mean to you?

When I think of a noble life, I imagine a life that sets an
example for others. The word noble is not often used today,
which makes a modern definition somewhat problematic.
But a noble life is one that is good, and I would say that
we should all aspire to a good life.

**As chairman of Hospice UK, what role do hospices
play in ensuring a noble life?**

One word which comes to the fore in terms of what
hospices provide at the end of people's lives is dignity, a
word that many people associate with noble. Providing
dignity is a big objective but hospices do it very well –
they are incredibly uplifting places with a real upbeat
atmosphere, which is not necessarily what you'd expect.
The key to creating such an environment is simple –
hospices deal with people as individuals.

What role does nobility have for older people, particularly those nearing the end of their lives?

Let me give you an example: a man near the end of his life was initially reluctant to go to a hospice but was eventually persuaded to go. When he arrived, the first thing they asked him was: 'Sir, what would you really like?' He answered that he'd really like a bowl of porridge, whereupon he was given a bowl of porridge.

Another example: I recently heard a story about a woman very near the end of her life. Her granddaughter was in an advanced stage of pregnancy but her grandmother was very ill and it didn't look like she would survive long enough to see her give birth. The hospice brought in a scanner so that the grandmother was able to see an image of her unborn grandchild before she died.

These examples demonstrate that hospices provide such individual care because they take the time to – they can focus on giving people what they want, which sustains nobility. Treating people as individuals makes all the difference to ensuring that they can end their lives nobly, with dignity.

Are there any hospice staff members you've met who you think set a particularly noble example?

Every hospice staff member sets a noble example. They are remarkable people working in remarkable places. They show compassion, the ability to care and the ability to treat every person as unique. Here's another story for you: a few weeks ago I attended a hospice. It was half-past four on a Friday afternoon and the staff were taking round a drinks trolley. And why not? Small gestures like this can have a big impact and create a sense of enjoyment. Hospice staff go to great lengths to give people a better quality of life at the end of their lives – what could be nobler than that?

Lord Howard is a Conservative peer who served as Leader of the Opposition and the Conservative Party from 2003–2005. He is Chair of Hospice UK, which works to raise awareness of hospice care in the UK.

ALISON GARNHAM

Octavia Hill's desire to make 'lives noble, homes happy and family life good' still chimes with us today. For me, her vision captures precisely why, as a society, we should focus more on tackling the causes and effects of child poverty. The latest research on why some children fare less well in life, and suffer poor outcomes, points to low income as the single, largest predictor and causal factor, with parental stress the most likely key factor affecting children. A good upbringing, a happy home and the prospect of a noble life are all much more likely if a child gets a decent start in life and their parents are not stressed, tired and worried.

A safe and secure home is, for most of us, the unremarkable background to our happiest childhood memories. Imagine if, instead, your life experience is marked out by an insecure home, no money and exclusion from many of the activities and opportunities that your friends take for granted. Of course, all children need the basics – love, nourishing food and a roof over their head – but some essentials have changed over time. Today, in addition to the struggle to afford a decent meal, children cannot complete school assignments without access to the internet or without being able to afford school trips. Also, there is constant pressure to wear the 'right' clothes – clothes that don't attract the invective 'trampy' – and to participate in the latest social activities. We won't end this insecurity until we end child poverty.

And parents, too, feel the strain. One woman in a food bank in Bristol told me how her fondest wish was to get more than ten hours' work a week out of the supermarket she was employed by so that she would have more money to plug the hole blown in her rent by cuts to housing benefit. Her efforts to keep a roof over her child's head had driven her to the food bank because the money she'd set aside for food had to be used to cover the rent. I don't think it takes much imagination to see what effect circumstances such as these would have on a happy home and good family life, leaving aside for one moment the humiliation of having to resort to a food bank. Decent pay and hours would have been enough to transform her life – together with some benefit reform, of course! A decent income, a decent home and universal access to education and health are part of what makes a decent society. Furthermore, what we want for our children is not just for them to be a means to an end, to be productive citizens; instead, we want our children's lives and wellbeing to be seen as an end in themselves. Trying to make the best of one's life in the face of adversity *is* noble. Individual life, in itself, *is* noble. I think this is what Octavia Hill was getting at and how right she was.

Alison Garnham is Chief Executive of the Child Poverty Action Group, the leading national charity working to end poverty among children and young people in the UK.

JONATHAN, LEX AND MICHAEL

So, you were asked to brainstorm the concepts surrounding 'individual life noble, homes happy, family life good'. How did you do that?

Lex: We discussed the definitions of what each part might mean generally…

Jonathan: And then afterwards we discussed what the parts mean to us individually.

Okay. This idea of a noble life – what did that get you talking about?

Lex: I think it's different for different people. We often see things in accordance with our own world view.

Michael: I agree that being noble can have a different meaning for different people.

Lex: Words that spring to my mind include [reads from list] 'encouraging, supportive, wise, intelligent, energetic in expression and action'. Being noble can't be taught.

One of you mentioned the word loyal. How does being loyal make someone noble?

Jonathan: It's about being responsible. To be reliable and honest in what you do.

Michael: It's also about being comfortable in yourself.

Who do you know who sets a noble example because they are loyal, because they stand out or because they are confident?

Jonathan: My uncle is noble. He listens to your problems. I can tell him stuff that I can't tell anyone else sometimes.

Michael: My aunt is like that. I can confide in her.

Lex: One of my friends, a personal advisor, is noble. They used to help me get work experience and paid work. They were really committed to helping me and encouraged me to try any challenge. I felt like my life was in a dead end and I needed to get motivated. My friend gave me some options. All we can do is move forward.

What about being happy?

Jonathan: Enjoying yourself. Stable job, happy family, lots of fun. Smiling all the time!

Can any of you describe a time in your life when you remember feeling really glad that you had a happy home?

Michael: Christmas! Because I get to see all my family together.

Jonathan: Being with your family is important so you can share the things you've done or experienced.

Lex: I can tell you a story – I've never told anyone else before. One of my dad's sad stories is that from a young age he was a slumdog. His family were in the poorest area and they had a very hard life. He couldn't find work. He was a thief – he used to steal food to survive. That went on for many years until he got older, went to college, got a steady job and met my mum. It makes me think about what it really must have been like for him, to feel what it was like in his shoes. He never had any luxuries. But now he is in London he works, gets paid, supports my mum and that's it. He's happy now because he has us – me and my brother. He has been happy seeing us grow up and although we might not necessarily have the perfect job, we've had the chance for a better future. Life is still a struggle though.

So, what do you want from your family lives?

Michael: Communication, sharing, interaction.

Jonathan: Being able to do things together.

Lex: Going back to the idea of being noble, it's a lot harder to be noble without a home and a family isn't it?

Jonathan: Yes. A happy home life can give you the tools to help someone progress, achieve their goals, get what they want from life.

Jonathan, Lex and Michael regularly attend BASE, a free club for young people aged between seven and 21 in Pimlico, which is run by the Octavia Foundation.

DAVID HOLMES

In 1869, Octavia Hill co-founded the Charity Organisation Society (COS) which organised grants for the disadvantaged and pioneered a home-visiting service that formed the basis for modern social work. Some 146 years later, COS is now called Family Action. Today, in addition to making small financial grants to people in need, Family Action also provides a wide range of support to children and families through 125 community-based services across England.

Every day, through Family Action's work, I am reminded of how precious a good family life is and how desperately hard it can be to achieve for families who are struggling. We work with so many families where anxiety and depression, tension and conflict, parenting difficulties and, often, poverty combine with other stressful factors that make it extremely difficult to live what Octavia called a noble life. I am still deeply shocked when I witness the suffering of some – such as the family referred to one of our family support services where the mum was struggling to cope and her older boy had just been arrested for a violent assault. Caught in the middle was a little boy who showed his anxiety by urinating frequently in his bed and on his few toys.

Picture that boy and his family – theirs was not a noble life, nor a good family life, as Octavia envisaged it. Our job was to help the members of that family to address their problems by giving practical and emotional support. Remembering that boy motivates me to keep growing Family Action's work so that we can reach more children like him.

In early 2015 we published a report – *Opening Doors, Changing Lives* – which highlighted the positive impact that small financial grants can have on disadvantaged people. The people who received grants under the Open Doors programme spent the money on the basics of life – fridges, washing machines, pots and pans, bedding, towels, tables, chairs, heaters, flooring and curtains. But these grants not only enabled people to buy things that they needed, they also gave them some control in lives that had somehow been derailed. It gave them self-worth when they were at their lowest ebb. It helped to build resilience, trust and a sense of security in people who had lost hope. With a grant of just a few hundred pounds, or a service provided at just the right time, we can help people to glimpse a more noble, happy and fulfilling life, and a glimpse is often all they need to move forward with confidence.

I wonder what Octavia would make of poverty and disadvantage in modern Britain? I suspect she would agree that the types of philanthropic deeds through which she transformed the lives of the Victorian poor are now needed more than ever.

David Holmes is Chief Executive of Family Action, the UK's leading family charity which supports over 45,000 families and children through community-based services.

"THERE IS AN ARABIC PROVERB WHICH TRANSLATES TO: 'NO MATTER HOW POOR ONE IS, HE IS RICH IF HE HAS FAMILY.' I THINK THIS SUMS UP WHAT OCTAVIA WAS TRYING TO ACHIEVE IN SOCIETY."

Moktar Alatas

JASVINDER SANGHERA

or me, the concept of a 'noble life' is that all of us, as
human beings, whatever our circumstances, can recognise
the role we have to play in society.

I founded the Karma Nirvana charity in 1993 as a result
of my personal experience of fleeing a forced marriage at
the age of 16. I took the decision to run away from home. I
missed my family terribly and I no longer had any stability.
I was reported missing and found by the police but I
begged them not to send me home as my family would have
married me off, just as they did my sister when she was 15.

I called home, hoping my family would understand. My
mother was very clear – from that day I would amount to
nothing, I would end up as a prostitute on the streets – I was
dead to her. I felt like a perpetrator. I was homeless for two
weeks and I attempted suicide. I felt like half a person.

I had a secret relationship with my sister. She was forced
to marry. She eventually ended up in a love marriage but

suffered abuse and my family's view was that she should stay with her husband because of honour. She did, and in her early twenties committed suicide by setting herself on fire.

I became a campaigner because of situations like this. I recognised the need for a charity which gave a voice to my experience and hers. Through Karma Nirvana, I can channel my pain and my loss and allow it to help others live life beyond disownment and cultural imprisonment. Making your voice heard is what makes change; it gathers strength and momentum.

This year the charity is 23 years old. We have made a significant contribution to a pioneering new law and we deal with 800 calls each month. There is greater awareness of the realities of forced marriage and more survivors are sharing their stories. Countries such as Canada and Australia are now on the path to criminalising forced marriage.

My child and grandchild will never know their family on their mother's side. But they are free to embrace their own independence. Many women affected by forced marriage are told that if they leave they will be disowned. Or worse, they spend the rest of their lives looking over their shoulder in fear.

Interestingly, it is the people not affected by these issues who have helped Karma Nirvana most. It's about compassion and will. Our volunteers say that even if something doesn't affect them personally, they want to get involved because it is the right thing to do. They are from all walks of life. When we're recruiting, I tell people to bring compassion and we can teach the rest.

A noble person never forgets where they have come from. And they never, ever forget the cause. We are all just one part of the jigsaw. Real generosity towards the future lies in giving all to the present and this is beyond the financial as, importantly, it has to be about hearts, minds and the giving of time.

Jasvinder Sanghera is the founder of Karma Nirvana, a charity supporting women in cases of forced marriages and honour abuse. Her bestselling book *Shame* tells her story of avoiding a forced marriage.

MARC WOODS

My father wouldn't have realised it but he lived his life by Octavia Hill's rallying call to live life nobly and create a happy home with the family at its centre.

In his younger years my father was an air-sea rescue helicopter winchman. He would be lowered down to rescue drowning people from the freezing sea. Plucking people out. Returning them to safety.

Understandably, he had a healthy respect for water and it was because of this that my brother and I learnt to swim as a life skill – the fact that we later became good competitive swimmers was a bonus as far as he was concerned.

His family was the most important thing to him and this, combined with his fierce optimism, powered me through my cancer and amputation. He entered me into the disabled national swimming championships before I had even had my leg amputated and within 18 months I was swimming at the Paralympics for Great Britain.

His mantra of 'you can't do better than your best' eased me through the hard times and encouraged me towards more than my fair share of successes.

Undoubtedly, he wanted the best for his family but, critically, I was also brought up to 'give something back' and to 'do unto others as you would have them do unto you'. In short, I was raised to live decently, with integrity and with honesty. I was asked to consider if Octavia Hill's words are still relevant today and I would say, unequivocally, YES!

In an increasingly fast-moving age, in which we are encouraged to say as much as we can in as few words as we can manage, I call on Octavia Hill's words to be 'liked', 'hashtagged' and 'retweeted' for they are as much a relevant ambition today as they were 150 years ago.

Marc Woods is a former Paralympic swimmer, winning twelve medals, four of them gold, over five Paralympic Games. He was a member of the BBC Paralympic commentary team in 2012.

PETER TATCHELL

When I think of a noble life I think of the great human rights and social justice campaigners who have influenced and inspired me: Mohandas Gandhi, Sylvia Pankhurst, Martin Luther King and, to some extent, Malcolm X and Rosa Luxemburg. Each, in their own way, opposed orthodoxy and the status quo in favour of following their conscience and pioneering a new vision of society – as Octavia Hill did 150 years ago. They stood against the tide of public opinion with much dignity, often at great personal cost.

Yet nobility of thought and action is not confined to well-known public figures. When I contemplate the meaning of a noble life I also think of ordinary people who have done extraordinary things.

One such person is Allan Horsfall. Although not well known, he was one of the pioneers of the modern gay rights movement in Britain, with a campaigning record that spanned more than 50 years, beginning in 1958, when he joined the newly-formed Homosexual Law Reform Society (HLRS), established to secure the implementation of the 1957 Wolfenden Report, which had recommended the partial decriminalisation of homosexuality.

In Horsfall's view, the HLRS was too London-centric, intellectual and closeted. Supporters had no say. Allan saw the need for a democratic, down-to-earth campaign group that would take the case for law reform out into the provinces, where gay supporters could get involved and be open about their sexuality. Being out and proud was, according to Horsfall, one of the most effective ways to debunk prejudice.

In 1964, this man of modest background and means played the leading role in founding Britain's first grassroots, gay-led homosexual campaign group, the Manchester-based North West Homosexual Law Reform Committee, which was renamed the Campaign for Homosexual Equality (CHE) in 1971. Horsfall was the CHE's first secretary and later its president, a post he held from 1974 until his death in 2012. During his tenure, the CHE suffered vilification and setbacks but Allan remained undeterred.

When partial gay decriminalisation was won in 1967, the HLRS faded. Most of its supporters believed their goal had been achieved. Horsfall disagreed. Many aspects of gay life remained unlawful. Homophobic discrimination and violence was widespread.

Allan continued to push for change, showing remarkable vision and purpose. He was involved in the second wave of gay law reform from 1999 onwards, which ended the ban on gay people serving in the military, equalised the age of consent at 16, repealed Section 28, introduced civil partnerships, allowed same-sex couples to adopt children and gave gay people protection against discrimination. Crowning it all was the addition of the Sexual Offences Act 2003 to the statute book, which ended homophobic bias in the criminal code.

A warm-hearted, generous and much loved humanitarian, Allan Horsfall is a shining example of a noble life well lived. His story serves to demonstrate how, through the passion and commitment of individuals, society can be made a safer, more civilised and happier place. Individuals make a difference.

Peter Tatchell has campaigned on issues of human rights, democracy, global justice, environmental protection and LGBT freedoms for almost 50 years. He spearheaded the 2013 campaign to secure the legalisation of same-sex civil marriage.

SHAMI CHAKRABARTI

'Where, after all, do universal human rights begin?
In small places, close to home – so close and so small they
cannot be seen on any maps of the world. Yet they are the
world of the individual person; the neighbourhood he
lives in; the school or college he attends; the factory, farm
or office where he works.'

These words, spoken by Eleanor Roosevelt in 1958 on the tenth anniversary of the Universal Declaration of Human Rights, in many ways mirror Octavia Hill's ambition for 'individual life noble, homes happy and family life good'. As Director of Liberty, I often find myself speaking about rights in the context of the 'big issues' such as parliamentary bills, ministers' announcements and legal cases. However, our precious and fundamental freedoms are more intimate than that, they are the glue that binds people and democratic societies together. A glance at the newspapers on any given day reveals just how much we all cherish fundamental rights and freedoms, for ourselves and our families and for people like us – but not always for everyone else. But human rights aren't really as controversial as you might imagine and you really don't need a philosophy or law degree to understand them. They can be summed up quite simply in three words: dignity, equality and fairness. The greatest of these is equality, because there wouldn't be torture, slavery, grave privacy intrusions or suppressions of free speech or free elections anywhere in the world if we really upheld the value of equality. This is the greatest discipline in any democracy because it forces us to imagine what it would be like to be someone else – to be the person who is being oppressed, forgotten or cast aside.

Every human life is precious, no matter where it begins, and we are all of equal worth. And yet, sadly, these are challenging times for such notions. Some seem to have decided that these ideals, upheld by the rule of law, are simply too onerous and expensive in times of insecurity and austerity. But our small bundle of rights are far from trifling luxuries to be sacrificed amid strife. These values provide vital safeguards for every civil and political aspect of our lives, no matter how big or small. Do we want to be considered someone with a citizen's privileges or do we want to be someone with human rights? A world where rights are contingent on your nationality or immigration status will only protect you – and perhaps only temporarily – in a small corner of the globe. We have a choice to make – after all, in this shrinking, interconnected world of ours, we are all foreigners somewhere.

Shami Chakrabarti has been Director of Liberty, the British civil liberties advocacy organisation, since September 2003. A barrister by background, she is one of the UK's leading human rights campaigners. Her first book, *On Liberty*, was published in 2014.

ZAKIYA AMLAK

A s a youth worker, there are plenty of challenges – such as young people being stubborn and not listening. It can frustrate you. We are all human, but it's important to be able to turn a negative situation into a positive one. It can be difficult and it can take time, especially building up young people's trust and respect, but the reason that I like working with young people and children is because it's fun. Plain and simple, it really is fun.

I think that young people get stereotyped too much – for example, a couple of young people might do something stupid and then an entire group of young people will get called thugs, gang members or whatever. The media doesn't help the problem – it blows things out of proportion. There was a time when young people couldn't wear hoodies because people thought they were part of a gang, which is ridiculous. It's not just the media that's letting young people down – I think that education is letting them down too. Education right now does not seem to be enjoyable and that's not good. It's hard for young people around here: you're working and you're trying to save for your future. But the way it's going, it's like there might not be a future to save for.

In Octavia's time, a 'family' usually meant a mum, a dad, a couple of children and some extended family – a grandparent, an uncle, or whatever. In this day and age, families are not the same. Whether there is a mum and a dad, two dads, two mums, one mum, one dad, two grandparents or something else altogether, love is the strong thing that binds us. Octavia's desire for stable home and family life is as pertinent today whether we are part of a 'traditional' family or not.

What Octavia did for poor families and what she stood for was quite inspiring. If she hadn't been around, who would have helped those people? What would they have done? She wanted to change people's lives for the better and there is a lot that the government could learn from her. She didn't have to try and improve society; she didn't have to use her money to help the needy – but she did. That is a lesson that the government should take from her. Her ethos has survived for 150 years. Hopefully it will live on for even longer.

Zakiya Amlak is a youth worker at BASE, the Octavia Foundation's free club for young people. She is a resident of Kensington and Chelsea and has been involved in media projects run by the Octavia Foundation since she was 14.

JONATHAN G. OUVRY

O ctavia Hill lived at a time of great inequality between rich and poor. Nevertheless, she succeeded in making 'homes happy and family life good' for many disadvantaged people in Victorian London. As her great-great-nephew, I am extremely proud of the fact that Octavia's pioneering work and indomitable spirit inspired a long tradition of strong family ties and commitment to continuing her legacy.

In 1900 my grandmother, Octavia's niece Elinor Lewes (later Mrs E.C. Ouvry), was appointed a trustee of the Horace Street Trust, which had been formed by Octavia in 1886. It was much later, in 1961, when my grandmother was still a trustee, that it was decided to form the Octavia Hill Housing Association. By that stage my father, Romilly Ouvry, who had become a trustee in 1944, was Chairman. I became a committee member and its solicitor, and was appointed as Chairman when my father retired and assumed the role of Honorary President. For many years, the committee also included my uncle Norman Ouvry, my aunt Ursula Cash and my sister Genista Wheatley, who was also Chairman for a time. Thus, Octavia's work continued as very much a family affair.

Under the new name, many acquisitions were made and new properties were built. A substantial acquisition in the sixties was a large part of Wilsham Street in North Kensington, where some houses had been owned in earlier days, when the street had originally been called St Katharine's Road. It was a street of ill-repute and its name was changed so as not to put off possible tenants. It is difficult to understand quite how it can have been of more ill-repute than most of North Kensington at that time!

In her will Octavia left certain properties within the family, in particular Hereford Buildings in Old Church Street, Chelsea, which belonged to Mrs Cash before she gave it to the Trust, and Sarsden Buildings in St Christopher's Place, which was given to the Trust by the Ouvry Family Settlement. The St Christopher's Place properties, I'm very pleased to say, still remain a vital haven for low-paid workers in the middle of an extremely affluent and expensive area of London. Octavia would be pleased.

One of my most treasured possessions is a painting by Octavia, which depicts an old cobbler who was a tenant of a room in St Christopher's Place. He delighted Octavia, the label says, 'by his cheerful faith in the certain triumph of good over evil', a sentiment which resonates with Octavia's steadfast ambition to support the working classes to improve their lives in the face of challenging social and economic circumstances.

I often wonder what Octavia might think of today's lack of progress in housing equality and divisive government policies such as the bedroom tax. In such testing times, thank goodness for Octavia Housing and the Octavia Foundation, still continuing my great-great-aunt's work after 150 years. Long may they continue.

Jonathan Ouvry is the great-great-nephew of Octavia Hill.
He is a retired solicitor and lifelong Londoner.

THE COOT FAMILY

To have a happy home you've got to have compromise. That said, I remember once when we were painting our cottage – Dad wanted blue because he'd been in the Navy but Mum put her foot down and chose something different.

Family life has changed a lot. In the old days you could leave your door open and someone might pop round and say, 'I'm ever so sorry but can you lend me a cup of sugar?' or something like that. These days, we can only leave our front door open in the summer while we're sitting there, otherwise the police come round and say: 'You should shut your doors because there's terrorists around.' Actually, they didn't say terrorists – they said thieves! Thieves will break in if you leave your doors open and you're not in your front room.

The Coot family live in Red Cross Cottages, original Octavia Hill properties in Southwark built in 1887.

MARIA TORRES

N oble? Well, it's about being honest isn't it? Also, being kind and helpful. Helping people to get a step up the ladder, that sort of thing. Respect is important – if you don't respect someone, you can't expect them to respect you. Responsibility plays a part too. I used to do voluntary work for Age Concern – taking people on holiday for a week, that sort of thing – and through that I got involved with the Christian Alms Houses. After some substantial refurbishments had been carried out there, a number of the elderly residents did not want to come back so one of the bosses at Age Concern said to me: 'Maria, there are some empty flats at the Alms Houses. Would you like to move there and be the responsible resident?' I didn't know what a responsible resident was but he explained that it is a person who acts as a voluntary liaison person between the trustees and the residents. I agreed and he showed me around. I loved it! I loved the place and everything was gorgeous.

Back then I was young and healthy and I'd have tea with some of the old ladies if they were lonely, bring friends around, make sandwiches and things. I organised meals in the committee room and on the terrace and we used to make sure that the gardens were well maintained. As a responsible resident I contacted anybody we needed, like the plumber, the electrician or the man to fix the lift. I knew everybody and I loved looking after people. Community is important. Residents need to help each other but they also need to tolerate each other because we've all got funny ways. I'm in my eighties now and I have come to realise that when we are young we don't always appreciate what it is like to be old… so I am glad that I have been able to help older people over the years. Ever since I was a tiny little girl I have loved helping old people. Now I'm old myself. I never thought I would get to this age and be in a state where I can't do things for myself. I never thought it would get to this. I never thought I would live this long.

Whatever you want in life, just go for it because you will regret it if you don't. It is the only way.

Maria Torres is a retired nurse who has lived in Marylebone for 26 years. She is originally from Spain. After more than 25 years volunteering for Age Concern, she now attends trips to West End shows and concerts arranged by the Octavia outreach team.

"YOU KNOW, THINKING ABOUT NOBILITY, MAYBE THAT'S WHAT IT'S ABOUT. IT'S ABOUT HAVING A SENSE OF BELONGING AND A SENSE OF BEING WANTED, THE FOUNDATION FOR LIVING A NOBLE LIFE."

Lianne Joy

DR ROWAN WILLIAMS

'Nobility' is not a word that comes naturally to 21st-century lips – it sounds archaic, even pompous. We sometimes talk of the noble aims of a project, of a noble attempt at something (indeed, sometimes a noble failure), but find it very hard to use the adjective about a person. Can it be retrieved?

Nobility of aim or purpose seems to have something to do with integrity and the seriousness of an aspiration. A person may or may not achieve what they hope for in the moral world, but they can certainly look themselves, and others, in the eye and say they did what they could. Without a category like 'nobility' we risk imaginative laziness, as though no one could be that serious, or no ideal could be worth that sort of cost. And while this irony, pushing towards cynicism, seems radical or daring, its actual effect is conservative and oppressive. To have images of a life well-lived isn't to have artificial stories of heroism. It's to keep hold of a sense of the surprising and challenging in human life, and of the difficult truth that we just might be answerable for who we are and what we make of ourselves.

One of the saddest features of modern public life is the erosion of a sense of *honour*. It is – obviously – a sense that has roots in religious feeling, but it is not universal in religious people or absent from non-religious people. If we let it drift away, we shall find it easier and easier to accept for ourselves and (crucially) for others too a set of diminished expectations. And this means not only a more boring life, but one in which we become increasingly inured to cries of protest against inhumanity, unfairness and mean-mindedness.

I suspect that Octavia Hill referred to 'nobility' because she knew that without a sense of honour, accountability and answerability, we would offer our children's generation a gravely diminished world. And 'good' family life cannot be built on this sort of imaginative poverty. We need to think about what kind of relations within the family would express and nourish honesty, challenge us to grow up emotionally and imaginatively, give us the security to make mistakes and learn, and furnish us with the hope to become a person who can be trusted.

We worry, rightly, that we are passing to our children a depleted and threatened material environment. We should worry just as much about the damage to our moral and imaginative ecology that is caused by our failure to think honestly about character and honour – nobility, if you like. Who are our heroes, the people we think of as honourable? We'd better have some answers if we are not to surrender the imaginative field to celebrity rather than nobility, success rather than honest conviction or egotistical pragmatism rather than the struggle to become trustworthy.

Dr Rowan Williams is an Anglican bishop and theologian. He was elected as the 104th Archbishop of Canterbury in 2002, standing down in 2012. He is now Master of Magdalene College, Cambridge.

TAMSIN GREIG

I am sitting in the Red Cross Garden in south-east London, originally laid out by Octavia Hill in 1887 as part of her vision to encourage people to live 'noble lives'. The park has been recently restored to its original Victorian design, an oasis of wild flowers, meandering paths and a tranquil pond overlooked by six pretty cottages.

This oasis reminds me of a garden lovingly raised by my friend and neighbour, Albert Rawlinson, on the land that backs onto the railway line in Kensal Green.

Albert died this year. He was 100 years old, more than twice my age. I met him in 1996, already in his eighties then, but still active and energetic. I went with him and his wife Lilian every Thursday to do their shopping. They did everything together.

On my wedding day, as we were walking back up the aisle, Albert leaned over to me and whispered: 'Don't worry Tam, the first sixty years are the worst!' He was always playful and kind-hearted. The twinkle never left his eye, even in his last days when he was bed-bound and mute.

Albert worked on the railways all his life, starting at age 14. He married Lilian before the Second World War and they raised three sons in a one-bedroom flat overlooking the railway lines. Albert was the eldest of eight, served in the army during the war, helped build the local scout hut, was a churchwarden and became Head Ticket Inspector at Euston Station. He was loyal, practical, good-tempered – and was part of the community that welcomed and integrated with the influx of Caribbean families who moved into the area during the fifties.

But he never liked to talk about himself, and he never complained. Not even when they lost two sons to cancer, not even when they lost a grandson at too young an age. Not even when Albert lost his beloved wife to dementia.

My friend ended his days living in a lovely assisted-living apartment in a north London care home. In June 2014 they organised a celebration in the home to mark the 70th anniversary of the D-Day landings. Albert was the guest of honour. I arrived at the party to find him sitting in his wheelchair wearing a row of medals. He'd never thought to mention that he had been one of the Allied soldiers to land on the Normandy beaches. When I asked him why he'd never told me, he just shrugged. 'What was it like?' I pushed. After a short pause he said quietly: 'Terrible.'

It was only at his funeral that I learned that Albert had helped many of the injured victims after an IRA bomb exploded in Euston Station in 1973. Another act of heroism that my friend kept to himself.

Albert was an ordinary railwayman who showed extraordinary bravery through a century of extreme change. He loved his garden oasis beside the railway lines, he loved the teamwork of a 77-year marriage and he loved his ever-widening family. He lived an undocumented but deeply noble life, and the forget-me-nots he gave me from his garden to plant in mine remind me daily that a more noble life is ours to be embraced still.

Tamsin Greig is one of the UK's most popular comedy actresses. She has starred in *Black Books*, *Green Wing*, *Friday Night Dinner* and *Episodes*, and has recently appeared on the West End.

SHEILA ROCHE

Living in Marylebone used to be like living in a little village, it did. Knowing that people you knew were just around the corner – it was lovely. I had a neighbour, Flossy, who was, at one time, quite high up in the Salvation Army and when her mum died she looked after her Down's Syndrome brother. She gave up everything for him. But she still kept in touch with the Salvation Army and every Sunday the band would come and play in our courtyard. It was wonderful. You would open the window and throw the money out to them. We used to pay one and six a week to the good neighbours club and at Christmas you'd get a chicken, at Easter the children would get eggs and if anyone passed away there would always be flowers or a wreath. Life is not the same any more. I don't think things are good at the moment, at all. I hope that things get a lot better for my grandchildren and great grandchildren.

Sheila Roche is an Octavia resident living in Marylebone.

CATHY NEWMAN

Octavia Hill once spoke of the 'mighty issues of the new and better days to come'. Octavia, there is no shortage of mighty issues you would have liked to have grappled with in 21st-century Britain.

Let's start with everything you did to create happy homes. Today, home ownership is at a 25-year low, and the rate of house building is at its lowest since the 1920s. You would have had plenty to say about that.

Family life, which you did so much to improve, has also changed beyond recognition. Around a quarter of households with children are single-parent families, which poses significant challenges for social reformers like yourself.

And, finally, you were the living embodiment of successful social mobility. You had no formal education and yet you achieved so much for so many people. What would you make of the failure of successive governments to give children of all backgrounds the schooling and start in life they deserve?

These are mighty issues indeed and I hope that where you led, others will follow.

Cathy Newman is a journalist and presenter at Channel 4 News.

"IN FIFTY YEARS,
IF I LOOK BACK,
WILL I HAVE DONE
THE BEST I CAN?
IF I HAVE, THAT
FOR ME WILL BE A
NOBLE LIFE."

Zakiya Amlak

ACKNOWLEDGEMENTS

We would like to thank the following for their contributions.

The Rt Hon. the Lord Adonis • Moktar Alatas
Yasmin Alibhai-Brown • Zakiya Amlak • Osei Anane
Dr Elizabeth Baigent • Margaret Bailey • Natalie Bennett
The Rt Hon. the Lord Best • Akinola Beyioku • John Bird
Professor Dame Carol Black • Jane Bretherton • Leslie Brett
Lillian Bryant • Dave and Lorraine Burford • Mary Burns
Alice Caffyn • Beatrix Campbell • The Rt Hon. the Lord Carnwath
Shami Chakrabarti • Kam Chung • Peter Clayton • Lina Clifford
Helen Connolly • The Coot family • Eileen Crawford
Saskia Dakin • Gillian Darley • Alain de Botton • Dorothy Delahunt
Professor Paul Dolan • Philomena Dominique • Niki Durosaro
Boyd Emery • Dennis Flavin • John-Paul Flintoff • Alex Fox
Jonathan Franco • Alison Garnham • Mohammed Gbadamosi
The Rt Hon. the Baroness Greengross • Tamsin Greig
The Rt Hon. the Baroness Grey-Thompson • Michael Hagan
Isabel Hardman • Breda Hartnett • Ann Hawthorn • Ian Hislop
David Holmes • The Rt Hon. the Lord Howard • Sir Simon Jenkins
Lianne Joy Greta Kendall • George Lemos • Claire Levavasseur
Edmund Lewis • Tracey Louis-Fernand • Paul Mason
Sir Bert Massie • Deborah Meaden • Professor Duncan Maclennan
and Dr Julie Miao • Conceição Melo • Eva Mills • Martha Moran
The Rt Hon. Alan Johnson MP • Richard Mullender
Cathy Newman • John O'Callahan • David Orr • Jonathan G. Ouvry
Theresa Palmer • Maxine Peake • Grayson Perry • Charlie Phillips

Diane Phillips • Rita Powell • Lex Quiambao
Dame Fiona Reynolds • Sheila Roche • Campbell Robb
Max Robson • Jean Roch • Rosalind • Eileen Ross
Jasvinder Sanghera • Rita Shalom • Fariba Shirazi • Steve Smith
Debbie Sorkin • Beryl Steeden • Peter Tatchell • Sir Crispin Tickell
Gabrielle Tierney • Sandi Toksvig • Maria Torres • Julia Unwin
Keith Usher • Aldo Williams • Dr Rowan Williams
Peter Wood • Marc Woods

**We also thank the following for their involvement
in creating this book.**

Aliya Ahmad • Jean Alexander • Liz Allison • Kiana Arabpour
Bouchra Bakali • Teresa Ball • Steve Bartlett • Wray Bennett
Neha Bhatt • Josie Britt • Laura Brodie • Ed Brown • Andy Brown
Jurgita Cavedaschi • Bridget Clarke • Patricia Cooper • Lynne Dakin
Sue Dance • Anna de Souza • Elamin Elbeshir • Colm Ennis
Ricardo Erblon • Charmaine Francis • Janet Kiwang
Mary Gething • Eammon Gilligan • Kate Glinsman
Gwen Godfrey • Pooja Gosavi • Trish Halpin • Pam Haynes
Marian Hazzan • Jenni Heavingham • Craig Hill • Pat Hill
Nick Hopkins • Colin Hughes • Alicia Hyacinth • Alexis Jones
Elaine King • Jenny Liddiard • Andy Low • Lewis Lowe
Ian MacLeod • Tina Mazzoni • Neil McCarthy • Nader Mehravari
Dorothy Menon • Fatima Mohammed • Reena Mukherji
Sajda Munshi • Stacey Mwayuma-Swedi • Hishgee Nadmid
Mr and Mrs Noble • Ross Norman • Victoria Nzeribe • Tony Peters
Addison Redley • Chrissie Roberts • Hilary Rogers
Elizabeth Rowland • Solange Spyriadis • Vaniche Sweeney
Claudine Tyson • Andy Warman • Sylvia Warman-James
Emily Williams • Karl Williams • Jamal Williams-Skinner
Serena Williamson • William Wojtysiak

Particular mention must be given to Gillian Darley, who has supported the idea of this book from the outset; to Lauren Simpson, who calmly edited the pieces and helped sort us out an order of play; to Paul Roughan for his ingenious design ideas and for accommodating each new request we made of him so patiently; to Rachel Harrison, for keeping the whole thing going at times when we might have given up; and finally to Louise Ashwell who joined Octavia as an intern and whose energy, application and all-round organisational genius in coordinating pieces, interviewing contributors and making things happen, has been a pleasure to watch. Without her personal commitment this book would simply not have happened.

Thank you all.

The pieces in this book were all contributed freely. No one was paid. All of the costs of production were met from the association's commercial income and proceeds from sales will be used to fund activities for young people in North Kensington.

GH
September 2015